Multi-Systemic Structural-Strategic Interventions for Child and Adolescent Behavior Problems

THE *JOURNAL OF PSYCHOTHERAPY & THE FAMILY* SERIES:

- *Computers and Family Therapy*

- *Divorce Therapy*

- *Family Therapy Education and Supervision*

- *Marriage and Family Enrichment*

- *Treating Incest: A Multiple Systems Perspective*

- *Depression in the Family*

- *The Use of Self in Therapy*

- *The Family Life of Psychotherapists: Clinical Implications*

- *Chronic Disorders and the Family*

- *Women, Feminism and Family Therapy*

- *Circumplex Model: Systemic Assessment and Treatment of Families*

- *Family Myths: Psychotherapy Implications*

- *Aging and Family Therapy: Practitioner Perspectives on Golden Pond*

- *Children in Family Therapy: Treatment and Training*

- *Minorities and Family Therapy*

- *Multi-Systemic Structural-Strategic Interventions for Child and Adolescent Behavior Problems*

Multi-Systemic Structural-Strategic Interventions for Child and Adolescent Behavior Problems

Patrick H. Tolan
Editor

The Haworth Press
New York • London

Multi-Systemic Structural-Strategic Interventions for Child and Adolescent Behavior Problems has also been published as *Journal of Psychotherapy & the Family*, Volume 6, Numbers 3/4 1989.

The Haworth Press, Inc. 10 Alice Street, Binghamton, NY 13904-1580
EUROSPAN/Haworth, 3 Henrietta Street, London WC2E 8LU England

Library of Congress Cataloging-in-Publication Data
Multi-systemic structural-strategic interventions for child and adolescent behavior problems / Patrick H. Tolan, editor.
　　"Has also been published as Journal of psychotherapy & the family, volume 6, numbers 3/4 1989" — T.p. verso.
　　Includes bibliographical references.
　　ISBN 0-86656-974-X
　　1. Behavior disorders in children — Treatment. I. Tolan, Patrick H.
RJ506.B44M85　　　　1989
618.92'891 — dc20

89-26684
CIP

DEDICATION

To Meredith for constantly reminding me
of what deserves priority
and the importance of children in families.

Multi-Systemic Structural-Strategic Interventions for Child and Adolescent Behavior Problems

CONTENTS

Preface   xiii

Acknowledgements   xv

Introduction: Treating Behavior Problems from a
Multi-Level Structural-Strategic Approach   1
Patrick H. Tolan

Accountability in Family Therapy Involving Children   9
Lee Combrinck-Graham

Families and the Therapy of Antisocial and Delinquent
Behavior   29
Patrick H. Tolan
M. Ellen Mitchell

Principles of Family Therapy for Adolescent Substance
Abuse   49
Thomas C. Todd
Matthew Selekman

Treating Intrafamilial Child Sexual Abuse from a Systemic
Perspective   71
Sheila C. Ribordy

The Systemic Treatment of Bulimia   89
Richard C. Schwartz
Pam Grace

The Family School System: The Critical Focus for
Structural/Strategic Therapy with School Behavior
Problems   107
        Dennis E. McGuire
        Elina R. Manghi
        Patrick H. Tolan

Children with Chronic Illness: A Structural-Strategic Family
Approach   129
        Christopher J. Brophy
        M. Ellen Mitchell

Guidelines and Pitfalls: Applying Structural-Strategic
Approaches in a Multiple Level Perspective   151
        Patrick H. Tolan

Author Index   157

Subject Index   161

ALL HAWORTH BOOKS & JOURNALS
ARE PRINTED ON CERTIFIED
ACID-FREE PAPER

ABOUT THE EDITOR

Patrick H. Tolan, PhD, is Associate Professor of Psychology at DePaul University in Chicago, Illinois. His position there includes an appointment as a senior staff member of DePaul Community Mental Health Center, where he supervises family therapy training. He is affiliated with the Family Systems Program of the Institute of Juvenile Research and the Psychiatry Department of Michael Reese Hospital. He also maintains a private practice. A graduate of the University of Tennessee, Dr. Tolan was a postdoctoral fellow in Clinical Research Training in Adolescence at the University of Chicago and Michael Reese Hospital prior to accepting his position at DePaul. He presents and publishes regularly in the areas of family therapy, delinquency prediction, community psychology, and adolescent clinical issues. He is the co-editor, with Bert Cohler, of the forthcoming *Handbook of Clinical Research and Practice with Adolescents* and is an associate editor of *The Journal of Family Psychotherapy*.

Multi-Systemic Structural-Strategic Interventions for Child and Adolescent Behavior Problems

Preface

Quite a large number of family psychotherapy cases involve child and adolescent behavior problems, most often as presenting problems. Yet, few practitioners who specialize in treating these problems are trained in family therapy. Similarly, few family psychotherapists are trained in treating child and adolescent behavior problems. It is with special joy, then, that we welcome this important collection, which focuses on the interface of these two areas of specialization.

The purpose of this book is to provide the practicing clinician with an overview of structural-strategic approaches in family therapy for treating child/adolescent antisocial and delinquent behavior, drug abuse, eating disorders, sex-related problems, school behavioral problems, and problems with medical care compliance.

But in addition to providing an overview, this collection expands our knowledge and the utility of structural-strategic family therapy by emphasizing the role of responsibility and accountability of family members. Also, strategies for applying structural-strategic approaches in working with other systems is presented, particularly the school system.

Patrick Tolan is an associate professor of psychology and senior clinician at the Community Mental Health Center, DePaul University in Chicago. At the Center he supervises clinicians in training in addition to his own practice. He is affiliated with the Family Systems Program of the Institute of Juvenile Research, and the Department of Psychiatry at Michael Reese Hospital, in addition to his private practice as a psychotherapist specializing in treating children and adolescent behavioral problems within a family context. He is a former postdoctoral fellow in Clinical Research Training in Adolescence, University of Chicago. His most recent work is a forthcoming book, *Handbook of Clinical Research and Practice with Adolescents,* co-edited with Bert Cohler.

xiii

He has assembled an impressive group of colleagues in this outstanding collection. Among these fine contributors are: Lee Combrinck-Graham, MD, an internationally-known scholar in the area of family therapy and editor of a recent book, *Treating Young Children in Family Therapy* (1986, Aspin). She is currently Director of the Institute for Juvenile Research and Professor of Psychiatry, University of Illinois Medical School. Thomas Todd, PhD, is the Chief Psychologist at Chicago's Forest Psychiatric Institute, coordinator of substance abuse treatment at the Family Institute of Chicago. He is known internationally for his work in adolescent substance abuse, partially through his classic book with Duncan Stanton, *The Family Therapy of Drug Abuse*. Richard Schwartz, PhD, is Director of Training of the Family Systems Program, Institute for Juvenile Research in Chicago. He is also known internationally for his important books in the areas of family therapy treatment, training, and supervision. And Sheila Ribordy, PhD, is Professor of Psychology and Director of DePaul University's Clinical Training in Psychology for many years. She is nationally known for her methods of training and work with children and adolescent behavioral problems.

As a father of a 12-year old (Jessica) and a 4-year old (Laura) I am impressed with the utility of structural-strategic therapy for viewing and modifying children's behavior. My wife Marilyn and I are working on an effective intervention right now to modify our children's less than adequate room cleaning behavior! I hope it works as well as this collection fits together.

Charles R. Figley, PhD
Editor, Journal of Psychotherapy & the Family

Acknowledgements

The realization of any goal such as this rests upon the efforts of the contributors. I wish to thank each of them for their creativity and perseverance. The value of this volume is to their credit, the limitations are my responsibility. In addition, I wish to thank Charles Figley for his support of this project, Doug Breunlin for his consultation, and Betty Karrer for teaching me about family therapy and always impressing me with her grace. Although not mentioned by name, the numerous others who aided directly and indirectly in completion of this have my gratitude. As always, my wife Mellon, has been a superb colleague and a best friend. This project was supported in part by a grant from the DePaul University College of Liberal Arts. Our departmental secretary staff—Nancy Rospenda, Lucinda Rapp, and Loretta Carter are to be thanked for their expeditious deciphering of my notes and revisions.

Introduction:
Treating Behavior Problems
from a Multi-Level
Structural-Strategic Approach

Patrick H. Tolan

SUMMARY. The assumptions of a Structural-Strategic approach are outlined. The reasoning and value of a multi-level approach to applying these tenets with behavior problems of children and adolescents are presented. Also, the centrality of the concept of accountability is introduced.

Behavior problems of children and adolescents constitute the majority of referrals for psychotherapy of those age groups (Lessing, Black, Barbera, & Seibert, 1976; Tolan, Jaffe, & Ryan, 1988). In addition to the problems they directly perpetuate, behavior problems can also seriously impede use of educational and medical services. Thus, directly and indirectly, these problems comprise the largest proportion of many clinician's caseload and many "general" practitioners in fact "specialize" in treating such problems whether by conscious choice or dictation of referral patterns. At the same time, behavior problems are among the most recalcitrant clinical cases (Tolan et al., 1988). This predominance combined with the frustration engendered can leave therapists struggling or disillusioned about working with these problems.

For many of these problems family therapy seems to be the approach of choice (Tolan, Cromwell, & Brasswell, 1986; Tolan et al., 1988). However, despite this indication, there have been few

Patrick H. Tolan, PhD, is Associate Professor, Department of Psychology, DePaul University, Chicago, IL 60614.

1

guides for therapists wanting to use a family therapy approach to such problems. Those available tend to emphasize general theory with little specific actions described, or are merely a compendium of a variety of approaches without any conceptual synthesis, with interventions listed like recipes.

The present collection is designed to fill that gap by presenting a shared common conceptual basis (Structural-Strategic) but with each one providing specific guidance for intervening with one common behavioral problem. The papers address successively, antisocial/delinquent behavior, drug and alcohol use, sexual abuse, eating disorders, school problems, and behavior problems related to childhood chronic illness.

The approaches described all build upon the general theories of Structural (Minuchin & Fishman, 1981) and Strategic (Haley, 1980) to provide guidelines and strategies for conceptualizing, assessing, and intervening. In addition, the interventions described share, in common, two characteristics that expand the Structural-Strategic model. All use a multi-systemic orientation to conceiving of the problem, viewing family systemic interactions as only one aspect of the problem's organization. They also consider accountability of all systemic members/components essential to realizing the goals of the intervention.

THE STRUCTURAL-STRATEGIC APPROACH

Although often described as separate approaches to conceptualizing and intervening in family problems, the Structural and Strategic views share extensive conceptual bases and provide a complimentary set of approaches and techniques that can be quite effective with behavior problems. The approaches described here incorporate these in a hybrid fashion that utilizes Structural techniques for in-session change and Strategic techniques for out-of-session change. The model has been most fully realized at the Family Systems Program of the Institute for Juvenile Research in Chicago where this integration has been ongoing for several years (Breunlin & Schwartz, 1986).

The Structural-Strategic approach is characterized by several assumptions:

1. Family problems arise due to failure to adapt to situation or developmental demands that require shift(s) in the organization of the family. The goal of therapy is to help the family change interactions so they can adapt and progress toward and through normal developmental changes and/or adapt to situational demands. Behavior problems are symptoms that occur because they help maintain some systemic function by providing a partial solution to the developmental or situational demands. In turn, the problem behaviors are maintained by the systemic organization.

2. Two major assessment and intervention foci are the intra-familial hierarchy (parents in charge) and generational boundaries (family members have closer alliance with those of their own generation than across generations). Primarily, problems in adaptation occur when hierarchy is reversed or not existent and when boundaries are stronger within generations than between or are not differentiated between generations. Both problems are evidenced by intrusion of one system member into the behavioral domain of another or others.

3. Therapy is pragmatic and problem-solving oriented. The goal is to define a solvable problem that is a shared concern of the family and the therapist and to change family interaction patterns that occur around the symptom(s)' occurrence. By changing these interactions the symptom(s)' systemic function will cease and thus, so will the symptom(s). Changing minute by minute sequences as well as those occurring over several days are the primary foci. (Breunlin & Schwartz, 1986)

4. Although this approach recognizes the recursion between behavior and meaning, it assumes, primarily in regard to therapeutic change, that meaning is derived from action, rather than the reverse. If people can act differently they will feel differently. Why a problem occurred is of less concern than how it is to be solved. Explanations are seen as useful more for their metaphoric utility than because they can actually provide the "truth" about what happened.

5. The primary interventions are to interrupt or redirect behavior interaction sequences. This can be done by several methods. Three prominent interventions are enactments of brief familial

interactions that illuminate family structure (isomorphs; Minuchin & Fishman, 1981), reframing and redirecting family interactions' meaning (Madanes, 1981), and assigning out-of-session family tasks that require behavior that eliminates the need for the symptomatic behavior and/or changes the meaning of the symptom interaction relationship. (Haley, 1981)

Variations and further elaborations of these principles are available elsewhere and readers should be familiar with the general approaches to fully utilize the interventions described here.

THE MULTI-SYSTEMIC VIEW

In addition to sharing the Structural-Strategic base, the interventions described here all conceptualize behavior problems as developing and being maintained by multiple systemic level influence. The notorious recalcitrance of these problems may be explained by their multiple level determinants and the inadequacy of many therapeutic approaches to consider, let alone address, each of the constituent influences. All of the present interventions acknowledge that individual, family subsystem (marital, parental, sibling), family-extrafamilial, and community/social system organization are important impacts on the nature and course of the problem, and require consideration in therapeutic efforts. This view is more than merely noting that families are not the only level at which behavior is organized. It is recognizing the need to go beyond simply focusing on the family interaction and that family interactions can be reflections of more critical systemic organizations at smaller or larger levels. The tenets of Structural-Strategic approaches are used to intervene creatively, as needed, at several levels of systemic junctures. The concern is not with identifying where the problem lies, but rather with determining where intervention is necessary, most effective, and most efficient.

This acknowledgement also includes recognition that therapy of behavior problems always occurs within a given social context that has certain demands, constraints, and opportunities occurring. The effective therapist must be aware of these and know how to work within the resultant expectable parameters. For example, Brophy and Mitchell provide an examination of how to incorporate the physician-family relationship in enhancing compliance with medical requirements of children with chronic illness. Similarly, McGuire, Manghi, and Tolan argue for intervention of school problems primarily at the home-school level and offer specific suggestions about how to do this, given the constraints of school structures and modal family-school relationships.

The interventions described, although all recognizing multiple system influence, differ in the extent to which they emphasize intervention focused at a specific systemic level or component versus multiple component intervention. For example, Schwartz and Grace emphasize focusing on both individual internal system parts and the family while Todd and Selekman focus strongly on the family interactions and McGuire et al. focus specifically at the home-school level. Collectively, these papers suggest that the therapist must be able to assess multiple levels of problem organization and to be willing to include actions directed at different levels within the overall Structural-Strategic intervention.

ACCOUNTABILITY AND RESPONSIBILITY

The third commonality across these papers, and another shift from early Structural-Strategic formulations, is their emphasis on accountability or responsibility of system members or components. As discussed by Combrinck-Graham in her introductory paper, accepting accountability as a central aspect of therapy is critical to working with behavior problems. In fact, as suggested by Tolan and Mitchell, lack of accountability to others in the family or between system components seems to be the hallmark of behavior problems. In each paper, accountability and responsibility are central themes of the interventions, whether explicitly focused upon or implicit in the systemic shifts that the interventions promote.

This concern is approached in a manner consistent with the principle that explanation is not useful for assigning blame or getting at the "truth," but rather is helpful in developing the shared framing of how to solve the problem. Thus, as used in these papers, the terms connote how responsibilities for problem solutions shall be dispersed. Accountability emphasizes the interdependence of system members or components and implicitly has the assumption that all members are capable of helping with solutions. Blame is not part of accountability.

Traditionally, systemic approaches to behavior problems conceptualize behavior as systemically determined and not individually determined. This has led many to confuse accountability with blame or with therapeutic error (becoming inducted by the family to ally with one member against others). Therapists would block attempts by family members to make responsibility an issue in therapy sessions. However, as these papers illustrate, being accountable and responsible is an essential aspect of ending the behavior problem and yet, is quite distinguishable from blaming or becoming the ally of one member in their explanation of the problem.

Whether the responsibility is at an individual, family, institution, or social level, affecting change and maintaining gains requires that system members be able to fulfill their interdependent functions. This has several ramifications for therapy processes and many of these aredescribed in the papers included here. One important implication is that therapeutic goals shift from realizing a certain behavioral status to helping family and other important systemic members to engage in accountable interdependent problem-solving processes. In large part, this is a matter of helping them to act in a manner that holds members accountable for the responsibility of their roles but circumscribes the responsibilities by indicating those which are beyond each member's as well as the whole family's direct control. Accountability allows the problem to be solved, but provides a realistic estimate of what each member must and can do, while weaving the complex, interrelated, multiple-systemic changes that are necessary to ameliorate recalcitrant behavior problems.

CONDUCTING MULTIPLE SYSTEM STRUCTURAL-STRATEGIC THERAPY FOR CHILD AND ADOLESCENT BEHAVIOR PROBLEMS

This collection of papers is introduced with a conceptual discussion by Combrinck-Graham that advocates more careful and conscious incorporation of accountability into family therapy with behavior problems. This paper frames the more specific and technique oriented papers that follow and make up the largest portion of this issue. Tolan and Mitchell provide a discussion of family characteristics and contextual features that are essential in working with antisocial/delinquent behavior. They describe a conceptual argument for their approach and guidelines for how and when to utilize its components. Todd and Selekman update Todd's previous work in substance abuse to describe techniques applicable to a wider range of levels of abuse. By taking the view that such problems represent a condition akin to that which occurs in families with chronic psychosomatic disorders, they are able to highlight the structural, communication, and relational features that need intervention focus.

Ribordy summarizes the family therapy literature on sexual abuse, emphasizing father-child abuse. The reader is provided direction about how to engage and maintain a therapeutic relationship with the family while directly focusing on the family's responsibility to solve the problem. Schwartz and Grace expand Structural-Strategic models to include an intrapersonal systemic focus in addition to family work to enable eating disorder families to realize solutions to what is often considered the most difficult eating disorder to work with — bulimia.

McGuire et al. incorporate many techniques utilized in other school problem interventions but conceptualize this use as part of organizing the problem and intervening at the family-school level. They provide guidelines for evaluating the problem and directing interventions in a manner that emphasizes accountability and interdependence between home and school. Brophy and Mitchell summarize the empirical and clinical literature on issues in working with families of children with chronic illness. They provide an approach that utilizes Structural and Strategic techniques to intervene with the family, that incorporates constraints imposed by the caregiving system, to help facilitate the interface of the family and caregiving system. This approach can help get families of these children unstuck and move families and caregivers from oppositional stances to cooperation. Finally, Tolan provides a brief set of guidelines for work with behavior problems culled from the specific intervention articles.

It is hoped these papers can provide the reader with a congruent conceptual approach to the very challenging issues of family therapy with child and adolescent behavior problems, while providing specific and distinct techniques and emphases for the most common of these problems.

REFERENCES

Breunlin, D.C. & Schwartz, R.C. (1986). Sequences: Toward a common denominator of family therapy. *Family Process*, *25*, 67-87.

Haley, J. (1980). *Leaving home: The therapy of disturbed young people*. New York: McGraw Hill.

Lessing, E., Black, M., Barbara, L., & Seibert, F. (1976). Dimensions of adolescent psychopathology and their prognostic significance for treatment outcome. *Genetic Psychology Monographs*, *93*, 155-168.

Madanes, C. (1981). *Strategic family therapy*. San Francisco: Jossey-Bass.

Minuchin, S. & Fishman, H.C. (1981). *Family therapy techniques*. Cambridge, MA: Harvard University Press.

Tolan, P.H., Cromwell, R.E., & Brasswell, M. (1986). The application of family therapy to juvenile delinquency: A critical review of literature. *Family Process*, *25*, 619-649.

Tolan, P.H., Jaffe, C., & Ryan, K. (1988). Adolescents' mental health service use and provider, process, and recipient characteristics. *Journal of Clinical Child Psychology*, *17*, 228-235.

Accountability in Family Therapy Involving Children

Lee Combrinck-Graham

SUMMARY. This paper presents an approach to working with families of young children with behavior problems that emphasizes accountability as a way of clarifying the roles of therapist, parents, and, most importantly, children. The concept of accountability in relational ethics is presented and examined in clinical situations involving families with young children. Several examples are presented to illustrate how the concept of accountability clarifies the problems to be solved, what steps should be taken, and who should take them.

INVOLVING YOUNG CHILDREN

Historically family therapists and child therapists alike have been nonplussed by the idea of including young children in family therapy. Zilbach (1986) pointed this out when she found so few references to this work in the family therapy literature. Since her review, there have been a few more contributions specifically on the subject of young children in family therapy (e.g. Combrinck-Graham, 1986, Mazza, 1984, Wachtel, 1987). Madanes (1981, 1984) always includes young children in her work. But none of these authors has addressed the central issue of what prevents therapists from comfortably involving youngsters in the session — the unanswered questions of how responsible should they be held for the ongoing family process, how much should they know, and how

Lee Combrinck-Graham, MD, is Director, Institute for Juvenile Research, Associate Professor of Clinical Psychiatry and Director, Division of Child and Adolescent Psychiatry, University of Illinois at Chicago, 907 S. Wolcott Ave, Chicago, IL 60612.

much should they be involved. Grunebaum and Belfer (1987) summarize the child psychiatrists' attitudes when they observe that most of the child literature emphasizes advocating for children in the face of harm and exploitation perpetrated by their family members.

This paper is about accountability. In discussing this important aspect of interpersonal relationships, particularly in relation to young children in family therapy, it is necessary to address the accountabilities of children (which is the big question), their parents, and the therapist.

It is proposed that when a therapist considers the concept of accountability, he or she will more fully comprehend reciprocity as a function of the relational shapes that underlie family structure and family function. Then the roles of children in the family and in the therapy system become clearer. The points will be illustrated with case examples which are presented in some detail to demonstrate the level of participation, resilience, creativity, and understanding contributed by young children.

ACCOUNTABILITY

The term, accountability, was introduced to the family field through the Contextual theories of Boszormenyi-Nagy (Boszormenyi-Nagy and Spark, 1973, Boszormenyi-Nagy and Krasner, 1986). Accountability is one of the many finance metaphors that Nagy uses to characterize the relational system. Others include, "legacy," "trust resources," "balance of fairness," "investment," "entitlement," "revolving slate," and "ledgers." These terms connect with other key Contextual principles, notably "justice," to build a system of accounts and accountability which provide a framework for evaluating the "balance of fairness," in each relationship network. A fundamental principle of Contextual therapy is to be accountable and to hold others accountable; in so doing relational accounts, the balance of fairness between individuals, can be adjusted.

The states of being a child and of having emotional disturbance or mental illness generate a common response in our current social climate: these people are not accountable. They don't know any better; they are innocent of the effects that they have on other people and of the actions they undertake, either while a child or while under the influence of disturbance or illness. Our systems of care for children and of legal accountability are built around these principles. Children are to be protected from bad influences; other people are held accountable for influencing them. Children and mentally ill people are managed differently in the criminal justice system. Children have their own system, based on the premise that they are not legally accountable until a certain age. Mentally ill people have the right to plead "not guilty" by reason of insanity.

It may appear that the state of being a child is blessed, for normal consequences in response to certain acts are suspended. Yet there are consequences to this no-account view of children which are self-perpetuating and, ultimately, contribute to the destruction, rather than the protection, of these children. Some have even proposed that mental illness is really a state of incompetent unaccountability.

According to Contextual theory, everyone in a relationship system has obligations and is accountable for the fulfillment of those obligations. Even the very young baby has filial obligations—obligations to be loyal to those who gave him or her life and to those who sustain life through caring. The expectation of accountability is there, even at birth. This is the basis of reciprocity. The parents invest caring in the infant, and the infant returns their caring with filial loyalty; but in what form? By being soothed, by molding, by feeding avidly, and very soon by smiling and wriggling in response the baby will reward the caretakers' acts of caring.

When babies don't reward their caretakers in this fashion, it may be said that the baby is not accountable. Many babies are physically irritable and irregular so that it takes longer than expected for them to settle into a give and take reciprocal relationship. Some babies, such as those with sensory or cognitive deficiencies, or autism, appear to have specific relational deficits which interfere with their responsiveness. But many other babies and young children are not held accountable by their caretakers. The infant whose caretakers cannot tolerate any crying, who pick him or her up when crying begins and then complain that the baby does not sleep through the night is not being held accountable. Such an infant's states are over-read and over-responded to, and there may not be an opportunity for him to reciprocate.

Children's repertoires of accountability expand as they grow older. Obedience, responsiveness, and affection are early expectable levels of accountability. Verbalized responses, actions initiated to care for the caretakers, and moral responsibility are the later elaborated forms of children expressing filial attachment and loyalty.

Children, therefore, are accountable. But it is necessary for them to be held accountable in order for them to appropriately exercise their obligations.

In these terms the family can be seen as the system in which accountabilities are defined. In the nuclear family, parents have the *authority* to set expectations; they have the *right* to believe that those expectations will be met; and they have the *responsibility* to see that they are. Contextual theory posits that parents who have not been held accountable to their own families experience a distorted sense of personal entitlement which, if it is negative, will diminish their expectations of return from their children; if it is "destructive" it will increase their sense of right to exploit their children. Thus though parents have authority, rights, and responsibility, they are also *obligated* to set clear standards, to live up to those standards, to recognize and respond to their children's needs. In short, parents, too, are accountable. Children must honor their parents, and parents must be worthy of the honor. Each generation is accountable to the other in these ways.

What has been presented about accountability by the Contextual theorists as relational ethics are the principles by which generational boundaries are defined and maintained. In Structural family therapy, where boundary is a fundamental concept, generational boundaries are often mistakenly thought to represent power differential, so that the unsophisticated Structural therapist may approach family treatment of children's behavior problems by "empowering" the parents to overpower the child and control his behavior. But boundaries in Structural theory actually represent role differentiation. In these terms, the generational boundary represents role differences between parents and children. The boundary is the imaginary point of reciprocal exchange and accountability.

As the roles of both parents and children evolve through the life cycle, protecting and guiding young children which requires superior judgement, greater wisdom and experience, as well as physical control gives way to setting limits, as abstractions, and negotiating in a way that conveys respect for the judgement and strength of the youngster.[1] As children and parents evolve, their mutual accountabilities change, the nature of generational boundaries change, and so does the management of behavior problems.

CHILDREN'S ACCOUNTABILITY

It follows that children should be responsible for accepting the nurturance, education, and care offered by responsible caretakers. They reciprocate this care in the only way they can. The problem is that when children's rights are emphasized above children's responsibilities, children may threaten their parents, e.g., by calling the child abuse hot line when they have been reprimanded, spanked, or had some form of sanctions levied against them or by talking about suicide if things don't go their way. In this fashion, children ally themselves against their parents with unseen but willing social agents, and the parents either give in, under the threat, thus failing to hold the children accountable, or they escalate their disciplinary efforts to degrees that are actually abusive and validate the children's complaints. These types of parental response tend to weaken their positions with respect to their children.

Parents don't need to be intimidated by their children, but they often are. On numerous occasions I have seen an average sized mother stand up to a tall, strong teen-aged son, commanding his respect in sharp tones, and I have seen the son, physically strong enough to overpower his mother, meekly assent to her demands. I have also seen large and physically powerful fathers plead with their children to mind, helplessly retreating when the child defiantly sticks out his or her tongue and persists in the noxious behavior. It is not physical power, then, that prevails in these relationships. There must be a reciprocal recognition of accountability in which a mother exercises her authority and responsibility by setting limits, and a son honors his mother by responding.

When children suffer from physical, psychological, or other problems, much of their behavior is explained and excused as a consequence of these problems. Children and adolescents in mental health facilities are excellent examples of this. In one school connected with a prestigious mental health center, despite the skilled teaching from highly trained specialists, when a child refused to participate in class or acted up, it was assumed that the behavior had something to do with the child's therapy rather than what was going on in the present in school. Thus the youngster who acted up was removed from the classroom to talk things over with the therapist rather than being held accountable to teachers and his or her own learning. Similarly in many treatment centers children are excluded from school if they are too "upset" despite the fact that school is the daily work of children. It is the same attitude about disturbances in children that leads the staff in mental health centers to explain the youngsters' aggressive and antisocial behavior on the basis of emotional disturbance and to forget to let the youngsters know that these are not acceptable ways to get along in this world.

From the youngsters' side, this failure of being held accountable actually leads to a greater sense of anomie, powerlessness, and lack of control. Because their behavior is not taken seriously or personally, they begin to lose their sense of personal influence. Aggression and physical violence or self-injury may become the only ways in which they can express themselves interpersonally. Ultimately this experience leads to major distortions which are mistaken for delusions, thought disorders, or, in the confusion generated in the caretakers, borderline personality traits.

In younger children, this desperation which I am calling the failure to be held accountable, is often seen in the "monster" child syndrome. In this syndrome a child, often quite small, behaves in an infuriating fashion, testing, provoking, and continuing with such behaviors even after having been begged to stop. Such a child is described by their parents as uncontrollably bad, or as "hyperactive." "Is it possible," the parents inquire on bringing the child to a doctor, "that he has ADD?" The child, meanwhile, knows no bounds. He acts as if he is the center of the world; and there is much in his experience to confirm this belief. An example is Jonathan, an 8-year-old boy who began kicking his mother whenever she asked him to do something. Instead of setting limits, the parents brought Jonathan to a child psychiatrist, thinking that this behavior was a sign of emotional disturbance.

Jonathan's sense of invulnerability was expressed in his response to the therapists's question, "Who do you think is stronger, you or your mother?" Jonathan replied that he was, even when he stood up next to his mother, and she was bigger. When compared with his father, he still maintained that he was bigger and stronger. The father was asked to wrestle with Jonathan right in the office, but he kept letting him win, coyly remarking on how strong his son was. Finally, the father was urged to correct his son's distorted view of his own power by gently and firmly defeating him at wrestling. The whole family was in tears, father having wrestled with his conflict between what he saw as putting his son down and the need to give his son a proper perspective (hold him accountable); the mother with her fear that her husband would hurt the child; and Jonathan having lost his invulnerability. A follow-up, however, found Jonathan no longer kicking his mother and being more obedient. The parents were much more willing to set limits and hold Jonathan accountable, and the boy and his father wrestled every so often, so Jonathan could develop proper strength and skill.

PARENT ACCOUNTABILITY

Parental responsibility is defined differently in different families according to family tradition, ethnic and cultural experiences, and the personal experience of the parents. Debates over specific rules of parent conduct can be by-passed if the issue of accountability becomes the focus. Parents are accountable to provide clear and consistent expectations as well as consistent follow through in response to children's behavior. How well they do can be assessed by asking a series of questions. In what way are the parents accountable to their children? Is this way clear to them and to their children? And is there consistency to this accountability?

When parents are not accountable in this way a very common complaint about children is that they won't do as they are told. In response to transgressions of these sorts, children are punished in more and more extreme ways. Spankings or beatings are less frequently reported than grounding, restricting TV, and time outs. When children fail to mend their ways in the face of extraordinary measures (like a year of not watching favorite TV programs) it is more likely that there is an issue of parent believability than of child incorrigibility.

There are many ways to assess family accountability when a parent asks or tells a child to do something, and the child doesn't do it. A most straightforward way is to enact the scene. "OK, think of something you'd like Mary to do, here, and ask her to do it, the way you do at home. Mary, I'd like you to do whatever you do at home when your parents ask you to do something." There will be a few false starts as people get into their roles. For example the parents will ask for her to do something simple, and she does it. "Is that what she does at home?" the therapist asks the parents, in surprise, "Do it again, the way it goes at home." Finally they will get into a struggle, like the one at home, and the therapist sees how the child holds out in disbelief of the parents' intentions that she do what they ask. The therapist also sees that the parents have many reasons for not expecting their child to do what they ask: they may not agree on what is asked; they may not want to impinge on her rights; they may be intimidated by her refusal; they may feel that asking her is enough, and if she doesn't do it by asking, then she must have something wrong with her. In short, for a variety of reasons, they are not accountable for following through on what they requested.

This seemed to be the problem the Nolans were having with 11-year-old Ricky. At the therapist's request, they brought Ricky and their three little ones, Jamie, Randy, and Liza to the first session.

They complained that Ricky refused to do anything he was asked, was furtive, stole, and showed no remorse. The Nolans had tried all kinds of punishments. They had taken away Ricky's bike; they had taken away his television for weeks, months, and, finally, years. They grounded him for months at a time. They took away his Christmas presents, and they wouldn't let him eat with the family. And, in the face of all of this, they complained, Ricky didn't seem to care.

What really irked his mother was that she had a rule that he should make his bed before he left for school. Every morning, she sent him up to make his bed. Every morning, he said that he had. Then after the school bus had gone, she found that his bed was not made. What really irked Ricky's father was that Ricky made his mother so angry.

The therapist focused on making his bed, observing that since Ricky got away with it every morning he obviously didn't think his mother really meant for him to make it. Several questions were raised: Did the mother really want him to make his bed? Did he even know how to make it? The mother said that it was important for a man to know how to make a bed, even though when her son got married his wife would make the bed. But there would be times before he got married, when he would have to take care of himself. She felt that she should prepare him for that. On the other hand, when he did make the bed, it was always sloppy, and she had to remake it. Dad said, "He can make his bed and lie in it." The therapist was confused, so she turned to Jamie and asked if he had to make his bed. No. Did he think Ricky should have to make his bed? Yes. Why? No answer. Ricky, when asked about his understanding, shrugged his shoulders. "That's another thing that I can't stand," interjected the father, "He never answers; just shrugs his shoulders."

It seemed that at least Ricky and Jamie weren't clear about why it was important to make a bed. It wasn't clear to the therapist whether he was really expected to do so. So she asked, "How could you tell him that you want him to make his bed in such a way that he believes that that is what you really want him to do?" For the remaining part of the session, the parents tried to figure out how to let Ricky know they really expected him to make his bed, and the children evaluated the parents' proposed solutions.

This seemed to be an instance where the parents' inconsistency gave Ricky a message that it really didn't matter whether he made his bed or did any of the other things they asked of him. They were demanding, with no follow through. And, as the father illustrated with his gratuitous complaint about Ricky's shoulder shrugging, their complaints were so persistent and random, it was almost impossible for Ricky to know what was expected. The Nolan family returned for one further session. In that session, the parents went through a list of their expectations from Ricky, arranged them in order of priority, and threw out the things they didn't really mean. After that they felt good about working things out on their own.

THERAPIST ACCOUNTABILITY

The responsibility of physicians, therapists, and healers is a subject of philosophical differences. Extremes of difference are represented on one side by the rules of obligation to treat suggested by codes of ethics, such as the Hippocratic Oath. This viewpoint holds that the physician or therapist, through his or her training, has special powers and skills upon which the patient depends to get better. In this view, the therapist is responsible for assessing the problem, designing the treatment, and applying the treatment. The patient is to be receptive and compliant. The other extreme derives from the notion that healing is a natural process. The physician or therapist does not "cure" anyone, but helps the healing process along either through reducing impediments to healing, or by applying treatments which enhance healing. In this case, natural healing processes are responsible for the patient's improvement, and the patient, as a host, is as responsible for encouraging healing as is the therapist. The common ground upon which most family therapists define responsibility suggests a collaboration between patient system (family) and therapist. The therapist is accountable for activating healing resources within the family and the family is accountable for acting upon those resources for their own healing. This collaboration between therapist and family is based, however, upon differentiated functions and responsibilities, as the collaboration between parents and children is also based upon differentiated functions and responsibilities. Maintaining these differential but mutual accountabilities for the therapy process also represents a structural boundary between therapist and family system. It underscores the point that therapists are not organic to the family functioning; they do not manage someone else's children. If they do, they are confounding the boundaries of the therapeutic system.

The therapist's role follows directly from his or her position outside of the family system. This meta-position coupled with the therapist's training and experience enables the therapist to appreciate patterns of family relationships and behavior which can then be reflected to the family in ways that can be used by the family to preserve the patterns or alter them as seems fit. In order to discharge this responsibility, the therapist must maintain the meta-position while also joining the family members effectively enough to have these observations heard and accepted.

The therapist who is truly accountable recognizes the limits of his or her role and responsibility in order not to contribute to the incompetence of the family system. Within the framework of accountability applied in this paper, the therapist will be less likely to transgress on the family's own healing processes if he or she examines how the family system is accountable in treatment, and how the issues of accountability are managed within the family. Specifically, in what ways do parents and children hold each other and themselves accountable? In these terms, the therapist's responsibility is to assess and foster accountability at each level of the system in order to encourage effective boundaries and effective family organization.

The example of Sam and his family illustrates a standoff between child and parents that tempts the therapist to take sides, thereby becoming a part of the problematic system.

Sam, a nine-year-old only child, has been brought by his parents for treatment, because he is, in their words, "hopelessly bad." He and his parents are sitting with a family therapist. It is the first session, and the therapist is trying to find out about the problem.

The parents are relentless in their criticism of the child: he refuses to do what he is asked, pretends not to hear, stays out past dinner time without letting them know where he is, has bad table manners, doesn't do his homework, and lies about it. And recently he has been doing dangerous things like hanging down the stairwell from the third floor, and ignoring their protective commands not to do that.

Searching for strengths, the therapist tries to find out what the parents like about the child. But these efforts are in vain. The parents cannot say one thing, even grudging, that could redeem this youngster. He is bad; born bad; and will have a bad outcome.

The child is silent and downcast. He does not meet the therapist's gaze, seemingly hopeless that this experience will conclude differently from any others.

The therapist becomes desperate. He feels the force of these parents' words, authority, and pervasive negativism, overpowering the little boy who appears to shrink before his very eyes. He wants to elevate the boy; but he knows that if he takes the boy's side, all is lost. For the parents are likely to renew their attacks on the boy, and on the therapist.

Then the therapist asks himself a crucial question: "What has this child done to get his parents so angry with him?"

The question is addressed to the child: "You must be a very difficult boy that you get your parents so upset. How is it that they cannot find one nice thing to say about you?"

When the therapist confronts Sam with his responsibility for his parents' bad opinion of him, he begins a process of examining roles and responsibility for role functioning in families. The therapist's question may appear to be a strategic maneuver; indeed it may have a strategic effect. Sam's parents, hearing their son challenged and held accountable, may actually come to his rescue by attacking the therapist or by remembering some redeeming characteristics of their son. If not, the therapist may need to go on to wonder why the family with such a negative outlook stays together. This, too, may appear to be a strategic maneuver and may have a strategic effect. Those advantages and pleasures in being a family, previously denied, may now come tumbling out at the suggestion that they might not remain together.

But the important effect of the therapist's question is to convey that Sam is accountable; to convey this to Sam, and to his parents. By asking the further question, why a family who experiences itself so negatively stays together, the therapist conveys that the family is accountable; it is their choice whether they stay together, and how they stay together. Sam is accountable; the family is accountable, and, in keeping himself outside of their intimate relationships, the therapist is accountable to them.

In working with young children and their families, there are often moments similar to these. It is tempting for the therapist to quickly conclude that these parents have a stake in scapegoating their boy, possibly because of a bad marriage or because of some psychopathology in one or both of them. It is tempting to see the child as innocent, a victim of, if not malicious blaming, then, at the least bad parenting. If the situation appears like this to the therapist, then the likely course of action is to dismiss the child from treatment and to work with the parents on whatever problems they are having that interfere with their parenting. The therapist is likely to become a teacher and counsellor to the parents; the mode of work will be empowering parents. The effect will be that Sam will have no way of being responsible for his acts, and the parents will measure their own effectiveness by Sam's behavior, thus having no means for being accountable, themselves. If Sam's behavior improves, the therapist will be credited with good counselling. If Sam's difficulties persist, the parents will be blamed for not being effective with him. It would be difficult to predict which direction Sam's behavior would take, but, even if there were to be improvement, the "therapeutic" system is not an accountable system, and it is likely that the family will experience future problems and need to rely on outside authorities to instruct them in the solution. Very likely, whether Sam's behavior improves in this immediate situation, or not, he will become involved in delinquent behavior later. The parents will not blame him, but blame themselves. They will take steps to protect him from accountability, and the unaccountable system will be maintained.

Another course of action that could be taken by the therapist, is to work with Sam, alone, in an effort to rescue him from the negative atmosphere of his parents' criticism. This is not the usual course of a family therapist, but is not uncommon with child "advocates" in the mental health field. This choice does not hold the child account-able for how he relates to his parents, substituting the good, but part-time, understanding therapist for the real daily life experience of the family. Nor does it hold the parents accountable for balancing their input to their child with understanding and comfort. One might say that a therapist who chooses this approach is not accountable to the family system at all. Thus the likely outcome is that both child and family will continue to depend on the therapy to solve their problems.

This leads to a critical aspect of a therapist's responsibility, to activate accountable systems and to stay with the process to be sure that systems follow through on their responsibilities. Carrying out this responsibility has the greatest likelihood of reducing the usual outcome of lack of accountability, the possibility of chronic incom-petence, such as mental illness.

THERAPIST AND FAMILY ACCOUNTABILITY AND OTHER SYSTEMS

Therapists who work with children always encounter the family's involvement with other systems who have varying viewpoints on accountability. Since the general consensus has been that children are not accountable, there is a great tendency to find other excuses for their misbehavior or problems, excuses which, in the medical field, usually lead to a diagnostic explanation. The challenge for the accountable family therapist is to integrate these diagnostic state-ments into a plan of family accountability.

The example of Jeff is a complex illustration of work involving sorting out accountability in three generations in a situation where everyone tended to see Jeff as emotionally disturbed and therefore, not able to be accountable. A neurologist consulted with the family, but not with the therapist. The therapist then had the additional challenge of getting the family members recommitted to their mu-tual expectations and accountabilities.

> Jeff was four when he was brought for evaluation by his mother and maternal grandparents, with whom he lived, be-cause he was "emotionally disturbed." What other explana-

tion was there for his remorseless destructive behavior, throwing and breaking toys, throwing things at his grandmother, and letting forth a stream of foul words when anyone reproached him?

Jeff was a handsome youngster, stylishly dressed in Lacoste shirt and shorts and Nike sneakers. He obviously commanded great respect from his adult caretakers, who admired him, but stood aback from his activity. He tore into the office and began his four-year-old exploration process--examining all the objects and asking a flood of questions: "why do you have this, here? Whose truck is this? Do you have any children? Can I take this toy home with me?"

The therapist selected some drawing materials and told him that he could sit at the table and work with them, making clear that he was not to touch the things on her desk. She then asked his family to help him remember the limits. Soon Jeff was inching towards the desk, an eye on his mother to see if she was going to do anything, and another eye on the therapist, to see what she would do. The mother protested, "No, no, Jeff, the doctor doesn't want you to touch that." Jeff moved swiftly, picked up a photograph, and boldly asked the therapist, "is this your son?" "Je-eff," his mother protested from her seat.

Moving just as swiftly, the therapist grabbed the little boy and threw him over her shoulder, hanging him upside down by his feet. His response was a mixture of giggles and protests. When he began to swear, she immobilized hands and feet, and tickled him. Jeff's family gasped. "Jeff, don't hurt the doctor," they warned. Jeff tried to spit, so she tickled him some more, then deposited him in a folded ball on his mother's lap. Taking her cue, his mother caressed and restrained him, and finally released him to continue his own activity while they continued to talk. Throughout the rest of the session, Jeff tested, and either his mother or the therapist would playfully remind him that they were bigger and stronger and fully intending that he should be accountable to the limits we had set. At the end of the session Jeff recognized the therapist with a big hug and a kiss.

The therapist's physical intervention with Jeff may be seen as therapist non-accountability, as she intruded on his mother's domain. The object, however, was both to let Jeff know that when a limit was set in the office it was intended that the limit be observed and to demonstrate that Jeff could respect these limits; he could be held accountable.

> Troubles persisted at home, however, because Jeff's grandparents held his mother accountable for setting limits and punishments for him, but did not enforce those limits, themselves. That is, they did not wish to hold the child accountable for his own behavior. Things got a little worse, actually, because the grandparents expected the mother's management to produce results. When Jeff acted up, they attacked her, and so it went. At another whole family meeting the adults were charged to develop a collaborative plan. First they listed the things that they thought Jeff could be responsible for, the things they agreed they ought to be able to expect from him. These included his playing without destroying, his speaking about his anger rather than demonstrating it by hitting and throwing things, and his expressing himself without swearing. They agreed to a consistent response to transgressions which would be implemented by any adult in the family, banishing him to his room for a specified period of time. They also agreed that if he was loud or destructive while in his room, the length of time would be extended. They told Jeff their plan, he tested it, and they all found that it worked quite well. Jeff began attending kindergarten without significant incident. Jeff's grandparents rejoiced that he was not "emotionally disturbed" after all.

Sometime later, Jeff's mother took him to an appointment with a pediatric neurologist, which had been made months before. From her history, the neurologist determined that the child had Attention Deficit Disorder, and placed him on Ritalin. Suddenly, neither the child, nor his family members was accountable, because he had a diagnosis and a medication. This new view of Jeff took hold in school. The teacher viewed his behavior in terms of whether or not he had taken his pill, or how long it had been since he had had his pill.

The neurologist had performed a certain wizardry. In one session, he had confirmed the family's lurking suspicions about Jeff's emotional instability, had virtually undone a year's worth of work in reshaping the family members' responses to Jeff, and had then supplied a remedy in the form of Ritalin. He had also done this without collaboration with the therapist. This was consistent with a system having difficulty with accountability, and if the therapist had protested, to attempt to undo the neurologist's diagnosis, by disagreeing, she would be entering into a symmetrical struggle, in which the matters of accountability would become even more blurred. Instead she praised the neurologist's fame and reputation and rejoiced with the family that they had found a treatment that was so helpful in their management of Jeff. The task was now to figure out how could Jeff be a child who clearly benefited from Ritalin, and was still accountable for his behavior and actions. This meant reinforcing the family's and school's reasonable expectations, and sanctions when the expectations were not met, and working directly with Jeff's perceptions of his own control versus the control he might feel from the Ritalin.

With his mother present, Jeff was asked what difference the Ritalin makes. He was vague, at first. After a while, he observed that it slowed him down a bit. And what happens when he is slowed down? With some help from his mother, he admitted that this helped him to stop and think before he did something. When asked whether stopping and thinking was helpful, he thought it might be. Then who was doing the stopping and thinking, he or the Ritalin? Gradually, this five-year-old mind sorted out his own responsibility and how the Ritalin might facilitate his acting responsibly. Jeff's mother, in helping him to sort it out, was forming her own opinions. "Ritalin helps you to stop and think, and that's what we expect you to do. It may be harder for you to do that when you aren't taking the medicine, but after you've taken it for awhile, you'll know what it is like. We expect you to stop and think before you act, Jeff."

Jeff's further course was not entirely uneventful because of many changing relationships in his life. But a thread of accountability had been established which became a guide during some rocky times and which established in Jeff a sense of his ability to affect his own accomplishments and the responses he elicited from others.

CONCLUSIONS

Accountability is an important concept in therapy with children and families and the many systems they encounter as the children grow up. Keeping accountability in mind can be useful in the assessment of dysfunctional systems, and addressing accountability in therapist, family, and child, has corrective effects. People in all stages of development and in all phases of physical and mental handicaps can be and should be held accountable. It is reasonable, at the very least, to expect recognition of efforts of caring and response to those who make these efforts. Accountable behavior in parents insists on accountable responses from children. In order to create an atmosphere in which parents and children can negotiate these relationships with each other, therapists must resist taking over for the family, thus leaving them ample room for accountability for themselves.

NOTE

1. See Combrinck-Graham (1985) for a version of these boundary changes focusing on evolving family shapes through changing interpersonal closeness and distance.

REFERENCES

Boszormenyi-Nagy, I. & Spark, G. (1973) *Invisible loyalties*. New York: Harper and Row.
Boszormenyi-Nagy, I. & Krasner, B. (1986) *Between give and take*. New York: Brunner/Mazel.
Combrinck-Graham, L. (1985) A family model of development. *Family Process, 24*:139-150.
Combrinck-Graham, L., Ed. (1986) *Treating young children in family therapy*. Rockville, MD.: Aspen.

Grunebaum, H. & Belfer, M. (1987) What family therapists might learn from child psychiatry, *Journal of Marriage and Family Therapy, 12*:415-423.

Madanes, C. (1981) *Strategic family therapy*, San Francisco: Jossey-Bass.

Madanes, C. (1984) *Behind the one way mirror*, San Francisco: Jossey-Bass.

Mazza, J. (1984) Symptom utilization in strategic therapy, *Family Process, 32*:487-500.

Wachtel, E. (1987) Family systems and the individual child, *Journal of Marriage and Family Therapy, 13*:15-25.

Zilbach, JJ. (1986) *Young children in family therapy*. New York: Brunner/Mazel.

Families and the Therapy of Antisocial and Delinquent Behavior

Patrick H. Tolan
M. Ellen Mitchell

SUMMARY. This paper presents a structural-strategic approach to family therapy with antisocial and delinquent behavior in children. The approach is based on a specific conceptualization of antisocial behavior and emphasis on the essential legalistic-therapeutic tension that pervades work with these families. Assessment and intervention techniques and rationale are presented as well as attention to the use of skill-oriented individual therapy.

The purpose of this article is to describe a developing model of family therapy for families of children exhibiting antisocial-delinquent behavior. This approach combines components of behavioral and structural-strategic family therapy with individual sessions for the identified patient to enhance the emergence of more adaptive boundaries and alliances, clarify family processes, articulate shared family values and conflicts, and to build communication and social skills. Each of these activities and their corresponding effect on family interactions are seen as essential to ending the system maintaining function of the antisocial behavior (Tolan, Cromwell, & Brasswell, 1986).

The development of more adaptive boundary organization is essential to foster consistency of supervision and discipline by the parental system. This, in turn, permits the child's development toward independence. Focus on structural organization is critical for

---

Patrick H. Tolan, PhD, is Associate Professor, Department of Psychology, DePaul University. M. Ellen Mitchell, PhD, is affiliated with Illinois Institute of Technology.

shifting the family from defensiveness to shared values as well as tolerance for variations in family members' values (Reiss, 1981). It is important to distinguish current conflict from low cohesion. Adequate cohesion is a prerequisite to eliminating the need for the symptom of antisocial behavior. This process is promoted in family sessions through reframing and education as well as adjustment of boundaries between parents and children, between siblings, and between family and extra-familial systems (Minuchin & Fishman, 1981). The individual sessions aim at development and rehearsal of effective communication skills and promotion of concern for future ramifications of current behavior.

The system maintaining function of the behavior is seen as a product of the interaction of individual, familial, and extra-familial forces that promote the behavior and/or impede its change. Identification of these forces and how they impact on the family and treatment of these problems is a prerequisite to utilizing the intervention effectively and will be summarized here. In addition to providing the theoretical and empirical rationale for this therapy model, a description of the therapeutic components and their implementation will be provided. However, it is first important to specify how we conceive of and use the terms antisocial and delinquent because the definitions have implications for treatment. These terms have been used differently and interchangeably in the literature and therefore can be confusing.

DEFINING ANTISOCIAL-DELINQUENT BEHAVIOR

Delinquency is a legal term with psychological and treatment connotations implied, whereas antisocial tends to be a psychological and treatment oriented term with legal or quasi-legal implications connoted (Loeber, 1982; Mulvey & Phelps, 1988). Both refer to aggressive behavior by minors that transgresses the norms (laws) of our society and usually results in some harm to others. Implicit in each of these terms, and what we consider the essential systemic tension of work with families with this problem, is the pull between viewing the behavior as a legal/moral issue of discovering responsibility and assigning punishment versus viewing the behavior as a symptom indicating the presence of some etiological force that compels the child to act. This tension is present at each level of the therapeutic system. It can be observed within individuals, in family interactions, within the therapist-family system, and at the extra-familial and extra-therapeutic level. One way this is commonly evidenced is in the regular exchange at each systemic level about punishment on understanding as the optimal reaction to the behavior. Discussions that vacillate between extreme solutions such as institutionalization or dismissal of the problem as a phase that requires patience and understanding, reflect this tension.

"Antisocial" and "delinquent" have been used interchangeably as well as interchanged with terms such as aggressiveness, predelinquent, delinquent prone, criminal tendency, and conduct disorder (Lorion, Tolan, & Wahler, 1987). The present approach considers these terms to be synonymous and views antisocial-delinquent behavior as a continuum. This continuum includes behaviors which range from merely obnoxious "pesty" behavior directed at others, such as teasing, fighting, or refusing to cooperate, to those behaviors that are illegal but not necessarily serious, and as petty theft or skipping school, through serious criminal activity that has strong negative consequences for the victim, perpetrator, and family of the perpetrator. Thus, from this view, antisocial-delinquent behavior is not something committed by a few children at some point in their development. Instead, despite variation in form and extent, it is seen among all children throughout development (Loeber, 1982; Lorion et al., 1987).

Although antisocial behavior is evident throughout the lifespan, the appearance of patterned antisocial behavior prior to the preadolescent years is rare. However, prevalence rates computed from self reports are commonly over 50% for felony acts at midadolescence. Shortly after the adolescent years, prevalence rates drop to almost preadolescence levels (Gold & Petronio, 1980; Tolan, 1987). Even the majority of adolescents committing regular serious acts will discontinue.

Prognostic assessment can be difficult. It is particularly difficult with adolescents, because delinquent behavior is so common. Thus, if level of current behavior or seriousness of the reason for referral are relied upon alone, it will be difficult to differentiate between adolescents exhibiting transient behavior that is an undesirable by-product of developmental problems from those evidencing a pattern of serious stable antisocial behavior problem that began early in childhood and which is likely to continue well into adulthood (Tolan, 1987; 1988b).

The Relevant Clinical Parameters

Despite the fact that incidence lacks definitiveness, there are useful and important ways to distinguish antisocial-delinquent behavior (Loeber, 1982; Lorion et al., 1987). These distinctions relate to the likely recalcitrance of the behavior and to the likelihood that the behavior is, in some form, a behavior exhibited by all family members. Understanding of the pertinent parameters is important for determining the need for therapy, and for distinguishing whether or not the behavior can be viewed as transient or representative of a chronic pattern. Each of these will require a somewhat different approach.

Determining what is clinically significant behavior from "normal" antisocial activity is difficult. Traditionally, the legalistic view has been that behavior that breaks the law and results in arrest is significant; the rest is not. The behavior is further distinguished by its legal seriousness (e.g, felony vs. misdemeanor). The therapeutic/medical view, classifies the behavior according to its duration which must usually be 6 months and by whether it was done alone or with others. From the present view, the behavior's significance is based on the extent and degree to which it is evident along five pertinent parameters: cross-situationality, frequency, age of onset, duration, and escalation, as well as the number of parameters in which problems are exhibited.

Cross situationality refers to the settings in which the behavior occurs. This can range from home, school, or work, to some combination. Seriousness is linked to a greater variety of settings. Similarly, frequency is an index of seriousness. Those adolescents committing acts periodically or "once in a while" are to be distinguished from those who violate rules and laws daily. The age when significant transgressions first occur and the greater the duration or past history are also important to assess. The longer the behavior has existed, the younger the child when it was first observed, the rate at which the behavior escalates, and the extent to which there is evidence of development of more serious or extreme acts, the poorer the prognosis. Multiple indicators of seriousness suggest a greater likelihood of legal intrusions which will constrain and intrude upon the therapy. Multiple indicators will also portend a greater recalcitrance of the behavior, a greater need for individual sessions and a slower therapy course in a population in which treatment is already difficult.

CONTEXTUAL INFLUENCES OF DEFINITIONS AND TRENDS

Despite these viable means for developing a sense of how therapy should be approached and how it is likely to proceed, the trends mentioned above can impact therapy in two other important ways. The first is that families and referring agents may attach prognostic meaning to the label used as the reason for referral. The term applied usually depends on the labeler's discipline and reason for contact, rather than any graded evaluation of seriousness or other meaningful distinction. However, as terms vary in the extent to which they imply a mental health or legal context for the contact, the "reason for referral" label can provide indications about the expectations of the referring persons. These referrals are almost always coercive; not at the child's and rarely at the family's instigation (Tolan, Jaffe, & Ryan, 1988; Viale-Val, Rosenthal, Curtiss, & Marohn, 1984). Thus, the referring person's orientation and view of the problem merits close consideration in implementing and conducting the therapy.

No matter what label is attached or how the case is referred, a dilemma of therapy will be in the tension between the legalistic/moralistic view of the problem and the treatment/psychiatric view. The former holds that the child does bad things for which s/he should be held responsible and punished. The latter regards the behavior as a symptom calling for treatment. However, as a "constituent" of the therapy process and outcome, the referring person's view of the problem is important because it indicates which view will be emphasized to evaluate progress and outcome.

The referral label can reflect contextual features which impact on treatment in many ways. When treatment is mandated as part of a judicial disposition or is a planned part of a defense, the impact is most obvious. The question of who is the client and whose interest shall guide therapy will color all therapist-client interactions. Disparities between the therapist's, the family's, and the legal system's goals for therapy will continuously disrupt therapeutic activities. Legal concerns and strategizing can engulf a child and his/her family and promote parents to seek extrication from the legal system rather than understanding of the family systemic meaning of the behavior and taking charge of the misbehaving child (Jurkovic, 1984). Therapeutic actions that conflict with legal concerns are likely to be undermined (Rappaport, Lamiell, & Seidman, 1980). The therapist may be seen as an agent of the legal system by the family while being seen as a biased advocate for the child by the legal system. Both roles impede the therapist's joining with and functioning within the family system. Each of these tensions occur in less explicit forms in any family therapy of antisocial-delinquent behavior, whether the coercing referring agent is the school, parents, or other social agent and need to be managed (Tolan et al., 1988).

The second implication of the proposed view of antisocial-delinquent behavior is that the prevalence rates among adolescents in general can obscure the seriousness of the behavior, its potential harm, and its meaning as a system regulating symptom. Parents and children will argue with each other and the therapist about whether or not the behavior (1) constitutes a serious problem and (2) whether or not "these problems" occur among their friends' and neighbors' families. The implication of these arguments being that if this is so, the problem is so widespread it is beyond the control of the family. Alternatively, it may lead to conclusions that it is not a serious problem and is best left alone. As the therapist, it is important to help disabuse the family of either conclusion and to instill hope for change.

THE FAMILY AND THE ANTISOCIAL CHILD

Although there has been a seemingly infinite number of studies and reports on the connection between family characteristics and the appearance of antisocial behavior, much of the literature is of limited utility. Two comprehensive reviews are available (Loeber & Stouthamer-Loeber, 1986; Tolan et al., 1986) and should be consulted if more specific and in-depth understanding of the state of the literature is desired. Both reviews underline a consensus borne out through a variety of theoretical writings and repeated empirical studies implicating family interactions and organization as the primary catalyst for the development and persistence of antisocial behavior.

Similarly, both reviews concluded that family status variables such as socioeconomic class, parental absence, or size are of little relevance once family interaction is considered. Thus (Tolan et al., 1986; Tolan et al., 1988), the literature converges to indicate that a family focus is primary in understanding the development of antisocial behavior and formulating interventions. Further, we suggest that the presented structural-strategic approach best addresses the aspects of the family system that are related to the antisocial behavior.

There are five characteristic differences in interactions of families with antisocial children which distinguish them from other families. First, these families are marked by long-standing and high frequency levels of parental conflict, especially around discipline and values directives to the children (Alexander, 1973; Hetherington, Stouwie, & Ridberg, 1971; Reiss, 1981; Singer, 1974). Most importantly, inconsistency occurs at the juncture of the parental-sibling subsystems, rather than within each parent. Each parent may be consistent in what they say to the children, but this may be at variance with directives issued by the other parent. Thus, the parental subsystem message to the children becomes inconsistent. For the parents, this often leads to alternating between identification with the antisocial child and sympathy for his/her struggle with the rules of the other parent, and feeling that the other parent is undermining their authority by not backing up directives to the child.

In the context of therapy sessions the parental interaction may appear to indicate an "underlying" marital problem that must be addressed to effect change in the child's behavior. However, proceeding in this manner and placing central and explicit emphasis on marital issues will almost certainly misdirect therapy, cause the parents to unify against the therapist, and perhaps lead to therapy ending (Haley, 1980). It is important to stay focused on the presenting problem(s) (Johnson, 1974). Probing the marital relationship in areas unrelated to discipline and coping with the antisocial child will usually reveal a great deal of agreement and marital strength. The strengths may be eclipsed by the stress of the current behavior management crisis and the ensuing demoralization of the family. The goal is not to resolve marital disputes, but rather to help the parents ally in behavior management to provide predictable and rational consequences to the child for desired and undesired behavior.

The second pertinent characteristic of the family interaction is a lack of differentiation in parents' and children's influence or power on family decisions and the direction of conversations (Alexander, 1973; Hetherington et al., 1971; Minuchin, Montalvo, Guerney, Rosman, & Schumer, 1967). A common pattern occurs in which the children are more influential than the mother in decision making, while paternal involvement is limited to erratic autocratic directives or extended diatribes of generalities that are not realistic and which are not the father's responsibility to implement or maintain (Singer, 1971; Jacob, 1975). This pattern calls for immediate and aggressive work to structure the hierarchy to increase parental power and strengthen generational boundaries. One way to initiate this is by instructing the parents speak to each other and formulate a rule about a discipline problem while requiring the child to listen without interrupting. Not allowing the child to intercede or be drawn into the conversation by a parent is critical. Often several repetitions of the enactment will be necessary before success can be achieved (Minuchin & Fishman, 1981).

The third characteristic pertains to the general lack of positive affect in family interactions. Family interactions are frequently coercive for all involved (Patterson, 1986). Positive expressions seldom occur and they are unlikely to be followed by positive responses (Alexander, 1973). Interventions which direct positive expressions are likely to meet with skepticism and heightened reactance or withdrawal by the family (Rorbaugh, Tennen, Press, & White, 1981). However, this issue can be approached indirectly albeit more slowly through discussion of respect which is a common theme among these families. It is evidenced by parents' complaints of lack of respect for their values and authority, adolescent's complaints of lack of respect for his/her struggles and the good things they do, and sibling complaints of lack of recognition for their self control. Initially, the therapist is best advised to ignore the negative affect and to help the family to ignore it as well. Positively connoting the motivation of each speaker, while attributing the negativity to limited communication skill can serve to accomplish this. The child can be coached to speak in a way that does not sound disrespectful, and parents can be coached to appreciate that a difference in opinion is not to be equated with disrespect or lack of affection. The focus on respect rather than being happy or liking each other is important; the positive effect will follow.

Fourth, communications in these families are more often misperceived and labeled as aggressive than in other families (Alexander, 1973). There is a heightened tendency in the entire family to be suspicious of the motivations of others and to assume intentional aggression. This propensity is usually more prominent in the identified patient. Systemically, this leads to less emotional cohesion, especially during times of conflict (Hanson, Henggeler, Haefle, & Rodicke, 1984; Tolan, 1987; 1988a).

Family problem-solving interactions are often viewed by members as threatening and as a situation of competitiveness rather than a joint challenge (Reiss, 1981). Thus, much of the communication is defensive and aimed at maintaining one's safety. Ironically, it is perceived as aggressive by other family members. This emotional atmosphere and set of family beliefs can create a family stalemate and therapeutic dilemma. Intervention requires determining who in the family is feeling good enough to move even minimally and thus end the stalemate. Most often it is the identified patient. He/she may be motivated to restore some of the previous trust, privileges, or peace whereas the parents are generally demoralized. The child can be told they will need to make the first step to get their parents to trust them again or to move to a more mutually respectful relationship. It is helpful to tell the identified patient they will have to make the majority of change. One technique we advocate is assigning a percentage of change, always more than 50%, as a metaphor for the effort the adolescent must expend. Thus, the identified patient is asked to initiate less defensive communications and more responsive behavior and to be patient if the parents do not respond. Assigning responsibility to the identified patient for systemic changes can be difficult and it is one reason for the importance of individual as well as family sessions.

The fifth important characteristic of these families is that a large percentage of communication time is dominated by one or two members with an implicit or sometimes explicit message of a lack of willingness to compromise. This can pull for the therapist to become too active by trying to speak for quieter members and negotiate between family members. However, learning to negotiate and learning that the interaction is the responsibility of the family is central to this therapy. Family determination of their own style is a requisite structural base for moving to a point that mitigates the need for the antisocial behavior. Therefore, it is important that the therapist not be inducted into the role of savior or shuttle diplomat.

The therapist should focus on supporting a functional hierarchy and helping the family to realize a more productive sequence of problem solving based on their naturally preferred approach. This can be accomplished through support of parental interaction to identify the primary concern(s) they want to communicate to their children. This will often allow compromise and an alliance between parents where it normally would not occur. It also serves to model compromise for the identified patient and other children. Another approach is to educate the parents about developmentally graduated rules, asking them to discuss and explain to their children what behaviors and freedoms are expected/acceptable at which ages. A third useful strategy is to structure the interaction time, giving 3-5 minutes for members to talk: first for the parents to voice their concerns, then for the parents to talk about commonalities and differences in their concerns, then for the children to react to the parental conversation, then for the parents to respond to the children's reaction, or the children to refine their reaction, and finally for the parents to determine and present a family rule.

A less direct manner of working with the family communications is to equalize the amount of time each person speaks during an interaction. This can be done by simply attending to what is said by those who speak little and interrupting those who speak continuously. Support and directives to reticent family members, along with instructions to be concise for those prone to speak extensively can also help. Similarly, vagueness and disillusionment are contents which signal communication ineffectiveness. For example, it is not uncommon for the mother of a delinquent child to speak forlornly about past closeness with the child, and wistfully suggest that if only they could once again speak freely the behavior would stop. She would need to be urged to specify what she means by talking freely and to articulate what she wants changed. When talking time becomes more evenly shared, especially between parents, the conversations tend to become more congruent. Congruency can also be nudged along by directing individuals to begin responses with what they thought of what was just said.

These five characteristics seem to be the primary systemic interaction qualities that distinguish antisocial families. The interventions for each, described above, constitute the primary methods and needed emphases of the therapy. Each requires recurring attention and modest gradual improvement rather than dramatic change. It is not possible to work exclusively on one area and then move to another when that area is "treated." The plodding process and need for shifting and recurring emphasis on the different areas with continued attention to hierarchical alignment can overwhelm the therapist. Therefore, it is usually helpful to circumscribe the focus of each session, while intermixing the emphases across sessions.

INDIVIDUAL AND EXTRA-FAMILIAL CONTRIBUTIONS TO THE PROBLEM

In addition to the central role of the family system in maintaining the behavior as well as the behavior's system maintaining function, individual characteristics and extra-familial contexts are major contributors to the development of antisocial behavior and need to be considered in interventions (Rutter & Giller, 1984). Individual influences need ongoing attention, while extra-familial issues need to be kept in consideration and attended to intermittently.

Three research findings about individual contributions are most robust and pertinent to the therapeutic approach espoused here. First, it appears that the relative propensity to be aggressive is one of the most stable traits humans possess (Patterson, 1986). Although the expression of aggression changes across the developmental stages (e.g., from physical toward verbal), compared to peers, *relative* level of spontaneous aggressiveness, tendency to perceive others as aggressive, and likelihood of responding with escalating aggression are fairly stable across the lifespan (Loeber, 1982; Lorion et al., 1987).

This conclusion may be rejected by many family therapists as antithetical to the family focus or as failing to recognize some underlying familial determinant of such behavior. However, the evidence is to the contrary. It is important to recognize that this tendency contributes to a bidirectional influence between the family and the individual tendencies in the development of antisocial behavior. The child's greater propensity resonates with and exacerbates any familial propensity (Loeber, 1982; Lorion et al., 1987). Failure to recognize this can lead to misinterpretation of parental reports and parent blaming that will alienate the family. For example, the parents will often report that the behavior seems to occur at slight or no provocation. They may report that the child has always been less responsive to discipline or less responsive to others' needs. The bidirectionality of influence can explain these reports and its recognition permits the therapist to respond in a manner that is congruent with the family experience. This is essential for construction of a shared workable reality to guide the therapy.

Second, it appears that lower social/interpersonal skills are more common among more aggressive children. Lower social skills is particularly predictive of serious antisocial behavior (Lorion et al., 1987; Pentz & Tolan, 1983). Again, the influence appears to be interactive, with poor social skills exacerbating aggressive tendencies, familial contributors, and social (extra-familial) inducements leading to significant antisocial behavior.

Clinically, this finding becomes significant in two ways. First, as the child's limited social skills will often lead to adjustment problems across settings, the parents may come to therapy viewing the problem as primarily within the child or beyond the family. Parental skepticism is frequently voiced about carrying out family focused therapeutic directives because the problem is not regarded as located within the family. The therapist is viewed as misguided in his/her emphasis on family change. This can lead to a loss of faith in the therapy, destructive outside consultations, or unilateral termination by the parents. The social skills limitations need direct acknowledgement and work in individual sessions.

The other impact of limited social skills is that in the familial sessions, which can be quite difficult in general, the identified patient is likely to be the most contentious and rapidly escalate to inappropriate behavior. This usually occurs because the child has limited skills for emotional expression and understanding of social interactions. Individual sessions that help the child to express his/her concerns productively, by coaching the child on how to get the parents to listen and how to make him/herself clear are needed. Without this the family sessions are likely to progress too slowly and/or chaotically for the family to remain in therapy.

The third clinically relevant finding is that antisocial children evidence less concern about the impact of their actions on others and their own future (Lorion et al., 1987). In the past, children were considered amoral and therefore untreatable. Alternatively, this observation led family therapists to dismiss the child from responsibility for their behavior and focus on the parents as the cause (Combrinck-Graham, in press). Both extremes are limited.

This issue is often the source of a frequent repetitive nonproductive sequence in which the parents focus on the child's lack of concern for others and other moral failures, while the child focuses on how he/she is being expected to give up his/her needs simply to fit his/her parents' "narcissistic" image of what a child should be. Neither side can alter their behavior for fear this would allow the other to escalate. The goal is to get one side to soften a bit and allow some modification of the perception of the other. Simply giving information about the child's tendency to overlabel acts as aggressive to the parents often helps them to be more patient with the child and to be more specific, consistent, and clear in directives. However, the primary manner of instigating change is to promote the identified patient's responsibility to lead in family change. As implied before, this responsibility will be taken if it is presented for its instrumental value rather than a moral duty.

The most effective and lasting means of altering this tendency is to help the child to develop and/or articulate for him/herself and to his/her parents a sense of future goals and to focus on how their behavior promotes or impedes realization of that goal. Individual sessions that use modeling, imagining antecedents and consequences of self-centered and impulsive actions, and behavioral rehearsal of how to talk to parents about desires for the future will facilitate development in this area. As the child masters these skills, the delinquent behavior will become less prominent as a means, albeit indirect, for discussing the future. At younger ages the content of individual sessions may focus around extracurricular activities or carrying out of family responsibilities and accessing family privileges, whereas for adolescents, the focus can be constructed around educational and vocational plans and goals (Shore & Massimo, 1979). The importance of giving this aspect of the problem consideration is evidenced by the fact that perhaps the only empirical evidence of successful individual therapy with delinquents focused on this aspect of individual functioning (Shore & Massimo, 1979).

Four extra-familial contexts are most relevant to the therapy of antisocial behavior. Two already discussed are the referring person's view of the problem as needing to be held morally responsible or receive treatment (Mulvey & Phelps, 1987), and the engulfing impact that involvement in legal proceedings can have. The other two are the influence of socioeconomic status and peers.

The socioeconomic influence is not one of differences in family interactions by socioeconomic status, but rather differences in access to economic and social resources. Poorer families have fewer alternatives for resources to solve family pressures and enhance the identified patients prognosis than richer families. This constraint can limit the options for the family and the therapist.

Peer influence is important for the therapist to consider because diminishing antisocial behavior usually involves a shift in friends as well as ways of relating to peers (Tolan, 1988a). Often friends are an area of contention between the identified patient and parents and any shift in this area occurs reluctantly. However, continued involvement with antisocial peers decreases the likelihood of maintaining therapeutic gains (Tolan, 1988b). The therapist must be able to maintain a balance of promoting the child's selection of friends, while helping them be responsible for "going along" with those getting into trouble. Parents can be supported in their concern, encouraged to establish ground rules about time with friends, and setting requirements that they meet all friends. However, it is essential that they come to view their child as responsible for their behavior whether they are the instigator or follower.

THERAPY PROCESS AND STAGES

As alluded to in general and explicitly mentioned in specific instances, the approach advocated here utilizes a combination of family and individual therapy sessions to emphasize change in five main aspects of the family that maintain and are maintained by the antisocial behavior. The process of therapy tends to be characterized by plodding progress with regularly occurring setbacks that can be demoralizing to the family and the therapist.

Progress is rarely straightforward or complete. It is best to warn the family of this initially rather than try to explain it after the fact when credibility will be severely diminished. Progress is evidenced by less serious, less frequent behavior problems in fewer settings. The interpersonal atmosphere of the family becomes less volatile and members less defensive and negative with each other. Although contentiousness often remains, it is slower to appear, less likely to escalate, and recovery is more rapid.

Another potentially demoralizing aspect of the process of therapy with these problems is that the therapist's help is rarely acknowledged, while availability and power are expected. Just as the family has trouble expressing positive affect with each other, they have trouble acknowledging it to or from the therapist. A grudging recognition that things are not so bad is usually the most direct expression that will be given.

This therapy, like all structural-strategic therapy, progresses through stages. After initial joining and aggressive support of a more functional hierarchy followed by establishment of the identified patient's responsibility to initiate change, the five emphases are each worked on, throughout the therapy. Thus, this type of therapy has a long "middle stage" (Breunlin, 1985). The length can vary greatly, but usually runs weekly for about 6 to 9 months. The length is shorter for younger children and less serious problems.

The individual and family sessions should run concurrently. However, if financial or time constraints do not allow this it is best to start with individual sessions with about one in four sessions for family meetings. When progress in social skills, particularly the expression of anger and frustration about the family, and when a growing sense about the future occurs, then a shift to primarily family sessions is recommended.

Stopping is recommended when the family can negotiate a developmental or situational conflict without needing the therapist to intervene. This is often accompanied by the parents' acceptance of the child and a growing ability of the child to be more self evaluative and complex in their criticism of their parents. Periodic check-up sessions are recommended for about 3-6 months post therapy. Early in therapy it is advantageous to elicit from the family their expectations about how things must be for therapy to stop and to introduce the idea of process as a goal rather than specific behaviors. Periodic reconsideration of what is necessary for stopping should occur throughout therapy.

The following case study briefly illustrates the application of this therapy.

CASE EXAMPLE

One of the authors was consulted about a case and subsequently asked to provide evaluation. The family had been seen intermittently over several years for increasingly serious behavior problems of the eldest son. Current problems included lying, staying out all night, school failure (including a recent suspension), some alcohol and drug abuse, and a recent arrest for burglary. He lived with his parents and two younger siblings. The most important recent family event was the father's loss of his position in a corporate merger six months earlier.

The first question, "Tell me what the problem is" led to a barrage of snipes and accusations between the two parents and the identified patient while the two younger children cringed on the sidelines. The initial session was characterized by repeated contentiousness, intense anger between the child and his mother, and the father's complaints that neither made rational statements. In addition, the family was feeling under pressure to be in therapy due to their son's legal problems. The mother wanted individual therapy to help the son be more responsible (and to punish him), while the son insisted the parents (and particularly the mother) were the problem. The father seemed accepting of both views; unable to see greater merit in one. Here as in other interactions, he treated the mother and son as squabbling siblings. The younger siblings refused to comment when asked what they suggested.

When asked directly what *he* wanted, father hesitated and finally said he wanted his son to figure things out, as he was tired of giving him advice that was not heeded. This comment received the first nod of agreement by the mother of anything her husband had said. Apparently they agreed about being fed up with their son. However, in speaking with the mother later in the session it was clear she still had hopes for the family and wanted the close mutually dependent relationship she had had with her son when he was a child. The son wanted legal emancipation but had no plans to move out of the house if he was able to accomplish this.

A session was held with the parents in which a history of the problem and evidence of an otherwise strong marriage were obtained. Two individual sessions with the son revealed a tendency to perceive others as trying to take advantage of him as well as a willingness to say whatever he thought the therapist wanted to hear. However when he was angry this social veneer disappeared. He had little planned for the future except to escape from his parents' control and to try and get out of the charges pending against him. This time was also used to explain the need for his instigating change.

The formulation of the solution as one which was more the son's responsibility than the parents, but which required the parents to be very clear about the rules and expectations for their son, was discussed in a feedback session. Both parents were skeptical that their son would respond, but they agreed to try if he would attend individual sessions to do something about his irresponsible attitude.

Family sessions initially focused on having the parents discuss their expectations with each other and to then tell their son about them. The father was encouraged to speak up more about his own views. Initially when the mother would speak about her expectations for the son she would include a criticism of the father. Once this was blocked, the son would interrupt and fight with the mother or comment to the therapist about how unreasonable his mother was. The father was asked to direct his son to not interrupt his mother. Once these interventions were realized progress in the congruency and relative time speaking in family interactions emerged.

Meanwhile, the court had placed the boy on probation because this was a first offense and he was attending therapy. Each week the family session would begin with the parents' litany of what the child had done wrong and the parents' belief he was hopeless. However, after repeated prompts to speak about what they wanted their son to do in each instance, the complaints shifted to be more focused on the process of discussing and directing discipline. Concurrently, the son began to express his needs more maturely, and showed recognition of the conflicting views of others in his explanations. This latter change occurred for some time before being recognized as "real" by the parents. Several times, the son acted out, although in less serious ways, when he perceived they did not recognize his effort.

Therapy "plodded" for six months with several setbacks occurring, including mother walking out of one session because she felt her son was not being held responsible by the therapist for his rule-breaking, and the parents asking the therapist to help them press charges against their son because of his threats.

At about seven months the parents requested several sessions alone to discuss their differences. The marital nature of these differences was focused on only as it influenced parenting. It was decided their son had to live with parents who were frustrated and who felt limited in their ability to care for each other but who were managing that problem. Also, they were able to form a strong enough generational boundary to compromise about discipline and agree about how their son fit into their desires for their family. This enabled them to tell him their expectations clearly and consistently. After this his behavior became less troublesome, although he continued to skip school periodically and argue with his parents about privileges. After a period of one month of relative calm it was felt it was time for the family to stop coming as they seemed able to argue out their differences without feeling overwhelmed or becoming destructive.

A follow-up session revealed some continued disappointment with the son by the parents, and he with them but a sense of tolerance of each other and the differences they had. No further legal problems occurred and school work was passing to above average.

REFERENCES

Alexander, J. F. (1973). Defensive and supportive communication in normal and deviant families. *Journal of Consultants and Clinical Psychology*, *40*, 223-231.

Breunlin, D. C. (Ed.) (1985). *Stages: Patterns of change over time*. Rockville, MD: Aspen Systems.

Combrinck-Graham, L. (in press). Accountability in family therapy involving children. *Journal of Psychotherapy and the Family*.

Gold, M., & Petronio, R. J. (1980). Delinquent behavior in adolescence. In J. Adelson (Ed.), *Handbook of adolescent psychology* (pp. 495-535). New York: Wiley.

Haley, J. (1980). *Leaving home: The therapy of disturbed young people*. New York: McGraw-Hill.

Hanson, C. L., Henggeler, S. W., Haefle, W. F., & Rodicke, J. D. (1984). Demographic, individual, and family relationship correlates of serious and repeated crime among adolescents and their siblings. *Journal of Consulting and Clinical Psychology*, *52*, 528-538.

Hetherington, E. M., Stouwie, R., & Ridberg, E. H. (1971). Patterns of family interaction and child rearing attitudes related to three dimensions of juvenile delinquency. *Journal of Abnormal Psychology*, *77*, 160-176.

Jacob, T. (1975). Family interaction in disturbed and normal families: A methodological and substantive review. *Psychological Bulletin*, *82*, 33-65.

Johnson, T. F. (1974). Hooking the involuntary family into treatment: Family therapy in a juvenile court. *Family Therapy*, *1*, 79-82.

Jurkovic, G. J. (1984). Juvenile justice system. In M. Berger, G. J. Jurkovic, & Associates (Eds.), *Practicing family therapy in diverse settings* (pp. 211-246). San Francisco: Jossey-Bass.

Loeber, R. (1982). The stability of antisocial and delinquent child behavior. *Child Development*, *53*, 1431-1446.

Loeber, R., & Stouthamer-Loeber, M. (1986). Family factors as correlates and predictors of juvenile conduct problems and delinquency. In M. Tonry & N. Morris (Eds.), *Crime and justice* (Vol 7, pp. 84-102). Chicago: University of Chicago Press.

Lorion, R. P., Tolan, P. H., & Wahler, R. G. (1987). Prevention. In H. Quay (Ed.), *The handbook of juvenile delinquency* (pp. 383-416). New York: Wiley.

Minuchin, S., & Fishman, H. C. (1981). *Family therapy techniques*. Cambridge, MA: Harvard University Press.

Minuchin, S., Montalvo, B., Guerney, G., Rosman, B., & Schumer, F. (1967). *Families of the slums*. New York: Basic Books.

Mulvey, E. P., & Phelps, P. (1988). Ethical balances in juvenile justice research and practice. *American Psychologist, 43*, 65-69.

Patterson, G. R. (1986). Performance models for antisocial boys. *American Psychologist, 41*, 432-444.

Pentz, M. A., & Tolan, P. H. (1984). *Social skills training with adolescents: A critical review of time trends, dimensions, and outcome, 1972-1982*. Unpublished manuscript, available from the second author, Dept. of Psychology, DePaul University, 2219 N. Kenmore, Chicago, IL 60614.

Rappaport, J., Lamiell, J. T., & Seidman, E. (1980). Ethical issues for psychologists in the juvenile justice system: Know and tell. In J. Monahan (Ed.), *Who is the client? The ethics of psychological intervention in the criminal justice system*. Washington, DC: American Psychological Association.

Reiss, D. (1981). *The family's construction of reality*. Cambridge, MA: Harvard University Press.

Rorbaugh, M., Tennen, H., Press, S., & White, L. (1981). Compliance, defiance, and therapeutic paradox: Guidelines for strategic use of paradoxical interventions. *American Journal of Orthopsychiatry, 51*, 454-466.

Rutter, M. C., & Giller, H. (1984). *Juvenile delinquency: Trends and perspectives*. New York: Guilford.

Shore, M. F., & Massimo, J. L. (1979). Fifteen years after treatment: A follow-up study of comprehensive vocationally-oriented psychotherapy. *American Journal of Orthopsychiatry, 49*, 204-205.

Singer, M. (1974). Delinquency and family disciplinary configurations: An elaboration of the superego lacunae concept. *Archives of General Psychiatry, 21*, 795-798.

Tolan, P. H. (1987). Implications of age of onset for delinquency risk identification. *Journal of Abnormal Child Psychology, 15*, 47-65.

Tolan, P. H. (1988a). Socioeconomic, family and social stress correlates of adolescent antisocial and delinquent behavior. *Journal of Abnormal Child Psychology, 16*, 181-194.

Tolan, P. H. (1988b). Delinquent behaviors and male adolescent development: A preliminary study. *Journal of Youth and Adolescence, 16*, 317-331.

Tolan, P. H., Cromwell, R. E., & Brasswell, M. (1986). Family therapy with delinquents: A critical review of the literature. *Family Process, 15*, 619-650.

Tolan, P. H., Jaffe, C., & Ryan, K. (1988). Adolescents' mental health service use and provider, process, and recipient characteristics. *Journal of Clinical Child Psychology, 17*, 228-235.

Viale-Val, G., Rosenthal, R. H., Curtiss, G., & Marohn, R. C. (1984). Dropout from adolescent psychotherapy: A preliminary study. *Journal of the American Academy of Child Psychiatry, 23*, 562-568.

Principles of Family Therapy for Adolescent Substance Abuse

Thomas C. Todd
Matthew Selekman

SUMMARY. The primary purpose of this article is to provide the therapist with general guidelines for conducting treatment with families of adolescent substance abusers from a structural-strategic orientation. After a brief review of the general literature and research on family therapy with adolescent substance abuse, an outline of the structural-strategic model will be presented, followed by specific modifications for treatment of substance abuse with adolescents.

REVIEW OF THE LITERATURE

For the sake of brevity, we have organized the most relevant publications on adolescent substance abuse and family therapy into the following three categories: family characteristics, family therapy approaches, and family research studies.

Family Characteristics

Several clinicians and researchers have written about the role of family dynamics in the development and maintenance of adolescent substance abuse problems. Baither (1978) and Stanton (1979) have provided extensive reviews of the family therapy literature on adolescent substance abuse to date and can be consulted.

Reilly (1975, 1979, 1984) describes the faulty launching patterns

---

Thomas C. Todd, PhD, is Chief Psychologist, Forest Hospital, Des Plaines, IL and is affiliated with the Center for Family Studies/Family Institute of Chicago.

Matthew Selekman, ACSW, CCSAC, is Family Therapist, Des Plaines Valley Community Center, Summit, IL.

Please address reprint requests to Thomas C. Todd, Chief Psychologist, Forest Hospital, 555 Wilson Lane, Des Plaines, IL 60016-9990.

and impaired mourning issues in families of adolescent substance abusers. He sees drug dependence as the substance abuser's paradoxical solution to launching yet still remaining connected and loyal to the family. The substance abuser "pseudoindividuates" from his family system (Stanton, 1979; Stanton, Todd & Associates, 1982; Weidman, 1985). Substance-abusing families are often riddled with painful losses. The adolescent substance abuser sacrifices his own autonomy to help family members avoid the trauma of separation or loss (Levine, 1985).

A number of clinicians and researchers have focused their attention on parental behaviors which contribute to the etiology and maintenance of substance-abusing behavior. The major factors reported in the literature were the following: parental denial, parental inconsistency with limit-setting, overprotection, unrealistic parental expectations, parental vicarious gratification, and triangulation. Kandel (1973, 1974, 1975) found in her research with adolescent substance abusers that heavy abuse of street drugs was reinforced by parental and intergenerational influences. Huberty (1975) argues that the parents' marital difficulties serve a major etiological and problem maintenance role in families with adolescent substance abusers. Haley (1973) and Stanton et al. (1978) describe how substance abusers serve as distance regulators in their parents' marriages. The adolescent substance abuser's behavior may be a metaphor for a chemically-impaired parent's problem (Howe, 1974; Madanes, 1981, 1984).

Many of the papers reviewed here characterize the family structure of families with adolescent substance abusers as being highly enmeshed and lacking any clear intergenerational boundaries (Fishman, Stanton & Rossman, 1982; Kaufman, 1984, 1985; Levine, 1985; Reilly, 1975, 1979, 1984; Stanton, Todd & Associates, 1982). However Levine (1985) and Friedman, Utada and Morrissey (1987) point to the rigidity of the family organization.

Very little has been written in the literature regarding sibling role behavior in families with adolescent substance abusers. Cleveland (1981) attempted to identify and classify some common sibling roles she observed in her clinical work with adolescent substance abusers. Kaufman (1985) found that siblings in these families tend to fall into two categories, the "very good" and the "very bad." The good siblings are often parentified and highly successful. The bad group consists of fellow drug abusers whose drug use is collusive with the identified patient (I.P.).

Family Therapy Approaches

Our survey of the literature reporting family therapy with adolescent substance abusers indicates that a wide variety of family approaches and techniques have been used. The majority of papers clearly reflect a strong allegiance with the structural and strategic schools of thought. For example, Stanton, Todd and Associates (1982) demonstrated the efficacy of combining structural and strategic approaches with substance-abusing families. Fishman et al. (1982) and Piercy and Frankel (1985, 1986) discuss the importance of empowering parents and actively correcting the incongruent hierarchy that exists in the families of adolescent substance abusers. Selekman (1987) and Howe (1974) found it to be efficacious to employ the adolescent substance abuser as a co-therapist in helping collect important diagnostic material and assisting the therapist in resolving other family problems.

Ellis (1986) and Piercy and Frankel (1985, 1986) have developed integrative family therapy models which they believe incorporate the best elements from the major family therapy schools: structural, strategic, M.R.I., behavioral, and systemic interventions. Piercy and Frankel utilize assertiveness skills training as an important intervention late in therapy to help assist newly abstinent adolescent clients with fighting off peer pressure to use chemicals.

Joanning, Gawinski, Morris, and Quinn (1986) and Friedman (1974) employ ecological-systemic models with adolescent substance abusers and their families. These clinicians argue that in order to successfully resolve adolescent substance abuse problems, interventions need to be targeted on multiple levels beyond the I.P., including the individual, family, and community levels, with therapeutic interventions targeted at all three levels. Friedman emphasizes the importance of assessing the impact of larger systems on the I.P. and the family, recommending intervention in the I.P.'s school context, peer group, and possibly the juvenile justice system.

Szapocznik, Kurtines, Foote, Perez-Vidal and Heruis (1983, 1986) have found in their research work with Hispanic adolescent substance abusers and their families that a one-person brief strategic family therapy approach is as effective in enhancing individual and family functioning as a conjoint strategic family therapy approach with this population. Szapocznik and his colleagues also found that the one-person therapy approach was effective in sustaining improved family functioning at follow-up.

Family Research Studies

Friedman et al. (1987) found that therapists' perceptions of substance-abusing families contradicted the family members' views of themselves. Family members viewed their family systems as being rigid and disengaged, not chaotic and enmeshed as widely reported in the clinical literature. Hendin and colleagues (Hendin, Pollinger, Ulman & Carr, 1981; Hendin & Pollinger-Hoss, 1985) discovered in their research with adolescent marijuana abusers and their families that unrealistic parental expectations played a major role in maintaining this problem in the family. Hendin and his colleagues view the use of marijuana as an attempt on the adolescent's behalf to individuate from the family.

A STRUCTURAL-STRATEGIC APPROACH
TO SUBSTANCE ABUSE

Similar to the model developed by Stanton and Todd (1982), the approach outlined in this paper is "structural-strategic."[1] This means that the overall approach is "strategic" in Haley's (1980) sense, including the focus on the symptom and behavior around the symptom, the planned progression of stages of therapy from one dysfunctional stage to another before achieving functional behavior, and the use of directives. Many of the moment-to-moment interventions during sessions are more structural, such as the use of enactment within sessions and the focus on intensifying and resolving conflicts. Other "micro-moves" are more strategic in a para-

---

1. A note on gender: While we wish to avoid awkward phraseology, we certainly do not mean to imply that either therapists or substance abusers are consistently of only one gender. Consequently, we will alternate the gender of pronouns used to refer to each of these two categories.

doxical sense, such as the use of restraining and prediction of relapses and the use of paradoxical or Milan-style final interventions.

Examples of more paradoxical final interventions could include an ambiguous message that the I.P. should continue taking care of the parents, a "Greek chorus" debate on the dangers of change, or a directive that the I.P. should pretend to have the symptom while the parents try to detect the difference between real drug use and pretended use. (See Todd, 1981, and LaForte & Todd, in press, for details.) Examples of Milan-style final interventions which we have found useful include the "Odd day-even days" prescription (Palazzoli, Boscolo, Cecchin & Prata, 1978) and the "invariant prescription" of Palazzoli (Simon, 1987).

The therapy is goal-oriented and short-term. Data is gathered early in therapy, particularly concerning drug use and family interaction around drug use. As data accumulates in early sessions, the therapeutic team will attempt to formulate hypotheses linking the substance abuse to the family system. Based on these hypotheses and data, the therapist will develop outcome goals and intermediate goals and will negotiate explicit goals with the couple or family. (All of these points are discussed in greater detail in later sections of this paper.)

The therapeutic goals should be consistently related to the drug abuse, but they should also relate to broader issues, particularly to interpersonal issues. Marital and family issues should be linked to the overall goal of reducing drug abuse. When symptomatic improvement occurs, it is crucial to shift the emphasis away from drugs but to anticipate possible relapse. Finally, when symptom-reduction has been supported by important changes in the system, the therapist should gradually withdraw, giving appropriate credit to the patient and family system.

Course of Treatment

For the sake of simplicity, we shall divide therapy into early, middle and late phases of treatment. In the initial session, the therapist attempts to obtain a clear statement of the problem in concrete, behavioral terms and investigates the family's previous attempted solutions. It is also important to understand the family's expectations of treatment. We seek to identify early those aspects of family life in which the instigation of change will have wider repercussions, including family alliances, parental relationships, filial relationships, peer relationships, and family rules and mythologies.

By the middle phases of treatment, we should know how cooperative the family is, what function the symptom may serve, what patterns of behavior can be expected, and what avenues of change may be profitable. By this time it should be obvious where the strengths and weaknesses lie. Meanwhile, there is a constant evaluation of tactics and strategies in use and continued feedback to the family regarding progress.

Handling of the late stages of treatment depends on the degree of progress the therapist has made. If there has been progress, the therapist summarizes the gains and looks for ways to deal with unfinished business. She also reinforces new patterns of behavior and moves to terminate, with plans for follow-up contacts in the future.

If there has been little or no progress in the sessions, then the therapist looks for possible flaws. Since this lack of progress should have already been evident during the middle phase of treatment, presumably adjustments have been made, and new tactics and strategies have been tried. Finally, there is a move toward termination, even without progress. (In the latter case there may be a referral for further treatment.) At times, the move toward termination in itself may cause a family reevaluation which the treatment alone could not accomplish.

TECHNIQUES FOR INITIATING TREATMENT

The Relevance and Role of Family Members

Stanton and Todd (1981,1982) have emphasized the importance of the "non-blaming message" in the recruitment of the families of drug abusers into treatment. While it is true that the families of adolescent drug abusers are typically much easier to engage in treatment than those of adult heroin addicts, it is still important for the therapist to offer a rationale for the involvement of family members that is non-blaming. This message should be tailored to the particular clinical situation, and may involve any of the following elements:

1. It is always safe to stress the need for a maximum, coordinated helping effort on the part of everyone involved in the life of the substance abuser. While the therapist conveys the expectation that therapy can be helpful, the therapist should also make it clear that he "needs all the help he can get."
2. The therapist should imply a belief that the parents and other family members have a genuine desire to be helpful to the substance abuser. The therapist also notes that, despite this desire, they may not know the best way to be helpful, or they may try to help in ways that turn out to have the unintended effect of promoting drug abuse or undermining abstinence. (This is similar to the idea of "enabling.")
3. Similarly, the therapist should not imply an underlying motivation on the part of the parents and family members to see the patient fail and use drugs. Instead, it is better to imply that significant others learn to accommodate to drug use and its consequences over a period of time, and that they may be unprepared for the upsetting effects of abstinence. The analogy is made to a broken leg or physical disability—no one wants such a handicap and anyone would like to get rid of it, yet the person having the handicap and those around him may be unaware of the complex accommodations that have been made to the condition, which will be upset by a return to normalcy.

The abuser or another family member may propose some alternative basis for involvement in family therapy, such as improving communication, dealing with parental problems, or addressing problems of a sibling. The therapist should accept such contracts cautiously and regard such goals as secondary to the primary goal of reduced drug involvement. If difficulties develop with these goals or if dealing with these goals seems to be over-stressing the abuser at an inappropriate time in relationship to the drug treatment, the therapist should always be ready to abandon or postpone them. (See Todd, 1988, for detailed consideration of such timing.)

Engaging the Adolescent Substance Abuser

This section of the paper presents effective strategies for engaging adolescent substance abusers in family therapy. We have found that it is most advantageous for the therapist to provide the adolescent substance abuser with ample individual session time in the early stages of family treatment in order to help establish therapeutic leverage. By joining well with the adolescent substance abuser, the therapist will not lose the I.P. when empowering the parents, which is a particular danger in early stages, before the therapist has had time to support the parental system. Some effective joining techniques with adolescent substance abusers are: positive connotation, the use of metaphors, empathy, humor, therapist use of self, and familiarity with street language. The joining process will occur much more rapidly if the family therapist demonstrates a good grasp of adolescent culture, as well as the street names of drugs of abuse and drug paraphernalia.

Once the therapist has developed a good alliance with the adolescent substance abuser, the latter can be employed as a "diagnostic tour guide" of her family system (Selekman, 1987). The adolescent substance abuser can provide the family therapist with invaluable diagnostic information about the function of the substance-abusing behavior for the family system. Since the adolescent substance abuser is often entangled in the parents' marriage, the family therapist can learn a great deal about the quality of the marital relationship and possible parental chemical abuse. It is useful to explore with the I.P. what family problems are most troublesome to her. A "secret pact" can be made between the adolescent substance abuser and the therapist regarding the latter's taking over sole responsibility for the resolution of the family problems. Throughout the family treatment process, the therapist should also convey to the I.P. his commitment to serve as an advocate and arbitrator for the latter across generational lines.

With some adolescent substance abuse cases, the parents are initially unable to bring in the I.P. for family therapy. This may be due to the substance abuser's power in the hierarchy, or often because an overinvolved parent is being protective of the I.P. Although it is helpful to have all family members present in the first interview, all is not lost if the I.P. fails to attend. The therapist can take advantage of seeing the parents alone by using this time to empower the parents and begin to correct the incongruent hierarchy. Homework assignments can be given to the parents to help disrupt the dysfunctional family dance around the substance abuser.

The Milan associates have developed some very effective engagement strategies specifically tailored for resistant family members (Palazzoli et al., 1978). The paradoxical letter is an effective engagement technique which can be useful when the I.P. is absent for the initial session. In writing a paradoxical letter to a resistant adolescent substance abuser, the therapist should begin the letter by positively reframing the I.P.'s behavior as serving a helpful function for the family, such as a protective function for the parents' marriage. This is followed by a prescription that the resistant adolescent should continue the oppositional behavior by failing to show up for the next session. The letter should be worded to imply that refusal to participate in family therapy defeats the adolescent's own goals. The I.P. quickly discovers that it makes more sense to be present than absent from family sessions. Weeks and L'Abate (1982) provide several examples of paradoxical letters that can be adapted for use with a resistant family. While such letters cannot be expected to "cure" a family by themselves, they may be useful in dealing with potential impasses such as the absence of a family member or an early termination of treatment.

DATA-GATHERING

The guiding principle in data-gathering is to understand the interpersonal significance of the substance abuse. It is, therefore, important to obtain data that allows the development and testing of hypotheses concerning the role of substance abuse and factors that may maintain the abuse.

Initially, a good deal of the data will concern the drug abuse itself. The therapist should take a careful drug history, being alert to time periods in which there were marked changes in amount or kind of drugs used. Building on this base, she should attempt to obtain information which offers clues about interpersonal factors. What effects have there been on others? How have family members and others tried to help? What shifts in relationships have occurred?

Illuminating data in three major areas are needed: (1) *Function of the symptom*. What has happened in the family or marital system during periods of accelerated drug use, during financial or vocational crises, etc.? What has happened when the abuser has tried to reduce his level of use or "go straight?" In addition to the family, what other people seem to play crucial roles? (2) *"Solutions" which become the problem*. On a day-to-day basis, what do the abuser, the family and others do in an effort to reduce drug abuse? What is the usual effect? More historically, what previous treatment efforts have there been? What was the outcome? (3) *"Organizational" issues*. The therapist should learn what other helpers, formal or informal, are currently involved with the patient (and with the family). This is especially important when the patient has recently been discharged from a residential program. If other "treaters" are involved, what sort of "program" has the abuser been given? What is the program ideology, and how easy will it be for the family therapy to co-exist with the other components of treatment?

Finally, the therapist should not forget the other key figures who are not in attendance but may be important. If the interview is with an adolescent and the parents, how do the siblings and the extended family fit in? What do they know or sense about the drug abuse? With respect to the families of origin it is helpful to obtain basic information about who comprises the families and where the members are. How are they involved with the nuclear family? Is there any current or past history of substance abuse or other addictive behavior in other parts of the family?

FORMING AND TESTING HYPOTHESES

When developing hypotheses, it is important for the therapist and any team members to keep in mind that the goal is to develop hypotheses which are useful therapeutically, as opposed to searching for "truth." Many possibly interesting hypotheses will have limited therapeutic value. The most important hypotheses, therefore, will be those having to do with the current role of the symptom in the family or marital system and in other interpersonal systems. Next, in order of importance, will be those hypotheses having to do with other factors which may be maintaining the drug abuse. These hypotheses may include the role of other helpers, the role of peers and the school environment, economic issues, etc.

None of this is meant to imply that hypotheses having to do with historical factors are useless. However, they need to be connected with current reality and current therapeutic strategies and goals. If, for example, there are issues surrounding the death of a significant family member who was linked to the abuser, which Stanton (1981) has frequently found to be the case, the issue for the therapist is to connect this event with the present and find some way to deal with it, even symbolically.

GOAL-SETTING

The process of establishing and refining therapeutic goals is crucial to the structural-strategic therapy of substance abuse, a process which begins with the first session. If the abuser, parents, or other family members are demoralized, it may be necessary to "sell" them on the possibility that therapy will make a real difference. More typically, however, it is better in the first session for the therapist to take a more neutral and somewhat pessimistic position, especially if the abuser is newly abstinent and optimistic about therapy. Under these circumstances, the therapist (or, even better, the team behind the mirror, if one is available) will usually express some doubts about whether therapy will be helpful, and will send the family home to think and talk about it before the second session.

Typically, the formal goal-setting process begins in the second session. The stated goal of the couple or family is usually quite clear — to have the drug abuser stop taking drugs and stay off drugs. The therapist, on the other hand, will wish to establish goals in two major areas — the area of drugs and the area of interpersonal relationships, with a clear relationship between the two sets of goals.

As the therapy progresses, it usually develops that the family has difficulty translating their goals into action. The abstract idea of abstinence may be fine, but the realities of confronting the abuser or setting limits on him may be more difficult to achieve. Furthermore, as abstinence is achieved, other problems typically surface and may develop into new goals.

DEALING WITH SYMPTOMATIC
IMPROVEMENT AND RELAPSES

The handling of symptomatic improvement or relapse is far from simple. Changes in either direction must always be evaluated in terms of previous patterns of improvement, the stage of therapy, and the ideal stance of the therapist and other team members. Only after all of these factors have been considered can an appropriate therapeutic plan be developed.

When therapy is proceeding well and there are no mitigating circumstances, it is reasonable to expect significant improvement as early as the third or fourth session. When this improvement occurs "on schedule," it is crucial to consolidate the changes and shift to interpersonal issues. To consolidate positive therapeutic change, the therapist should usually adopt a stance of guarded optimism — that the changes appear desirable and real, but they may not last. If a supervisor or team is involved, they can act split on this issue, with the treating therapist supporting the change and taking an optimistic stance, while the team members or supervisor act more pessimistic and skeptical.

As symptomatic improvement occurs, interpersonal issues typically emerge. It is crucial for the therapy to begin to focus more directly on these issues. If the family is allowed to maintain an exclusive focus on the abuser and the possibility of a return to drug use, rather than focusing on more basic interpersonal issues, a relapse will typically occur.

The therapist has considerable latitude in influencing the stance taken by the family when a relapse or slip occurs. At one extreme, it may be appropriate to treat an early relapse as a major crisis, mobilizing the resources of the family to meet this challenge. Usually such a relapse has already been anticipated and planned for, and the relapse is the occasion for activating this plan.

In contrast, it is often desirable to treat a relapse later in treatment as a temporary slip rather than a permanent reversion to drug use. When the family has made solid progress, the therapist should convey the attitude that they already know how to cope with this temporary setback. Usually the relapse comes when the family is facing

an interpersonal crisis, with the relapse functioning to divert attention away from the interpersonal issues. The therapist must recognize this pattern and prevent this diversion from occurring, even
though it may also be necessary to deal with the relapse directly.

TECHNIQUES FOR ENDING THE TREATMENT

Reviewing Goals and Giving Credit for Change

Structural-strategic therapy is typically of brief duration.
Whether or not it is formally time-limited, it usually lasts 10 to 20
sessions, over a period of four to six months. Within the context of
such brief therapy, it is particularly important for the therapist to
review goals periodically and be prepared to terminate when goals
have been achieved. Even when goal-achievement is less than perfect, the therapist may wish to move toward termination if therapy
has reached a point of diminishing returns. Stanton (1981) has argued that it is important for the patient and family to receive most of
the credit for change. The therapist should only take credit as a
facilitator or catalyst, making it clear that the family has done the
real work. It is also dangerous for the abuser to get too much credit
for change, since this lessens the commitment of the parents to
maintaining the changes and preventing relapse. In this respect, it is
important to link drug improvement to changes made in interpersonal areas.

The family should be warned in advance that life may not go
smoothly and that future problems can be anticipated. It is useful to
review the problem-solving skills they have learned in the course of
therapy to create confidence that they can deal successfully with
future problems or crises.

As termination approaches, longer intervals between sessions are
appropriate. Usually the final sessions are treated more as extended
follow-up visits than as therapy sessions, e.g., having the family
come at monthly intervals to review progress and insure that there
has not been anyslippage. If therapy has ended ahead of schedule,
the family can be told that they have a few sessions "in the bank,"
in the event that any problems develop during the follow-up period.

CASE EXAMPLE

William, a handsome 16-year old, was referred for family therapy with one of the authors (MS) by his high school counselor due to his failing grades and coming to school heavily intoxicated on a variety of substances. Prior to this referral, William had received outpatient family therapy on two occasions, and had been hospitalized for nine weeks for chemical dependency treatment. The mother called the therapist shortly after discussing the school problems with William's counselor. Mrs. Smith began the phone conversation crying and sharing with the therapist how she has "failed her children as a mother." She reported that "all hell broke loose" after her older son Steven moved out of the home eight months earlier. The mother believed that William had begun heavy abuse of heroin, PCP, alcohol, and marijuana after Steven moved out of the home. William allegedly had been using chemicals since age 13. The therapist scheduled a family interview for later that week.

From the information the therapist had gathered in his phone conversation with the school counselor and the mother, the following tentative hypotheses were formulated:

1. The Smith family was stuck at the Leaving Home stage of the family life cycle (Haley, 1980).
2. William's substance-abusing behavior served a protective function for the mother by distracting her from her own worries and dysphoria around Steven's moving out.
3. An incongruent generational hierarchy existed in the family which placed William in a one-up power position over his mother.

First Session

Present in the initial family interview were Mrs. Smith, William, and his 14-year-old sister Michele. Mother was quick to point out how "brilliant" and "helpful" her daughter was around the house and that she had been an honor student. The therapist employed humor and street language as a way of engaging William. William was impressed with the therapist's familiarity with rock music cult figures and his knowledge of street culture. It was interesting to note how Michele spoke for her mother and interrupted William without being restrained by her mother.

After joining with each family member, the therapist asked a series of circular questions to develop a clear picture of the "family dance" around the presenting problem, to elicit information regarding differences in relationships, and to confirm or discard initial hypotheses. The therapist found it helpful to ask Michele to give him a "motion picture" of what all family members did when William came home "stoned." The following sequence of interaction occurs: Mother lectures William about the dangers of using drugs; William becomes defensive and yells at his mother; the Mother begins to yell and cry simultaneously; Michele intervenes as referee and tries to comfort both parties; William begins to cry and escorts his mother to her bedroom; finally, after everything returns back to normal, William goes to his own bedroom. After reporting this scenario, Michele openly admitted that she was the "family peacemaker."

To help determine coalitions around the presenting problem, the therapist asked William to rank on a scale from one to ten each family member regarding their degree of concern about his drug use, with a ten representing the highest level of concern. William gave Steven a 10, his mother a 9, Michele an 8, his biological father a 2, and himself a 9. It was interesting to note how high the rank was for Steven. Surprisingly, William included himself in the ranking task, which gave the therapist a good indication of his motivation to change.

Midway through the session, the therapist dismissed the children and met alone with the mother, in order to demarcate generational boundaries and initiate the process of empowering mother. The mother began by describing the many ways she had failed her children, being married three times to alcoholic men. The therapist provided support and empathy. In an attempt to redefine the problem and maintain maneuverability, the therapist shared his "crazy" notion that William's behavior might serve a "stress-regulatory" function for the family. The mother appeared to accept the therapist's relabeling of William's behavior by presenting a few examples of how William takes on "too much responsibility" for her problems.

The remainder of the session was spent exploring with Mother what adult resources she had available to assist her in parenting. Unfortunately, Mother's family lived out of state and most of her female friends were single mothers themselves. There was discussion of the need for outlets for Mother to pursue when her stressful nursing job and her parenting responsibilities began to get the best of her. She was given the homework assignment of doing "one nice thing" for herself over the next week.

The last fifteen minutes of the session were spent alone with William to help solidify a therapeutic alliance with him. The therapist began by complimenting William on his "courage and devotion" to his family by serving as the "family stress-regulator." The therapist then explored with William whether he had any worries or concerns about his family. William shared with the therapist that he thought his mother was "very depressed and lonely."

The therapist complimented William on being a "very sensitive and caring guy." William smiled and agreed to make a contract with the therapist regarding his "turning over a new leaf." This consisted of total abstinence from all chemicals and allowing the therapist to take responsibility for the family change process. William shared his feelings of ambivalence, and the therapist discussed this ambivalence and concluded the session by predicting that William would struggle to remain "straight" over the next week.

Second Session

William began by proudly reporting his ability to remain "straight" for a week. William also shared how he fought off peer pressure to smoke "weed" with his friends. The therapist deliberately responded with disbelief and confusion. This was followed by a few "Go slow!" messages. The mother denied seeing any signs of drug use on William's behalf. Michele responded with pessimism around William's sudden change in behavior. Whenever Michele spoke for her mother, or talked to her brother in a maternal way, the therapist challenged her power in the family with comments like: "How old are you? Are you sure you are not sixty-four?

That's very interesting . . . How did you get so old in this family?'' These provocative meta-comments served to empower the mother and move Michele back into the sibling generation where she belonged. The mother admitted that she had virtually abdicated her position of authority in the family when Steven moved out. As she put it best: ''I went to the sidelines and watched Michele and William take over.''

After dismissing the children, the therapist quickly followed up on Mother's homework assignment. Surprisingly, she had done two ''nice things'' for herself, buying a new dress and registering for aerobic classes. The therapist complimented the mother on being so ''ambitious.'' The mother shared that she planned to continue taking ''better care'' of herself from now on. Sensing that a relapse was inevitable, the therapist restrained the mother from moving too quickly.

The therapist decided to utilize the last twenty minutes of the session with the sibling subsystem. Like William, Michele was very concerned about her mother's mental health, and she was eager to do anything to help Mother. The homework assignment given to the children was to be placed totally in charge of ''Mother's happiness'' for one week. This included having each child do ''one nice thing'' that their mother would notice per day. On Friday night, they were instructed to prepare an elaborate candlelight dinner for her. Both Michele and William were excited about their homework assignment.

Third Session

The Smiths came into the therapist's office smiling and laughing. Mrs. Smith reeled off a long list of positive things her children had done around the house. The mother was most touched by the wonderful dinner her children had prepared, followed by the showing of a home video that the mother had been dying to see. Mrs. Smith reported that she painted the family den single-handedly, a house project that had been discontinued after Steven moved out. The therapist praised the children for doing a ''fabulous job'' of helping out their mother. He played dumb and explored with the children what had come over them to be ''so super responsible and loving.''

Both Michele and William shared with their mother how much they "cared" about her. No signs of drug use were reported, but the therapist concluded the session by predicting that William was due for a relapse. The rationale given to the family was that "change is three steps forward and two steps back."

Fourth Session

As predicted, William came into the session with "bad news" about a relapse over the past week. William had smoked a marijuana joint and drank one beer. The therapist normalized the relapse by pointing out how it served as a "springboard" and "a building block toward further changes." The family was very supportive and provided William with encouragement to get back on track again. The therapist explored with the family how they responded to William's relapse. Mrs. Smith had contemplated giving William a severe consequence, but instead had him clean the entire garage. According to the mother, "the garage is now cleaner than it has ever been in the past." The mother reported that she was getting in "great shape" from her three times per week aerobic classes.

In concluding the session, the therapist shared with the family how he and his supervisor (TCT) did not always agree on client progress. He pointed out to the family that his supervisor thought that William would start using "hard drugs" again in the next week or two. The therapist took the pro-change position by telling William that he was "doing real well" and how he thought his supervisor was "nuts." William responded to the supervisor's challenging remarks with "your supervisor is full of crap!" The therapist shook hands with William, and they both agreed to work together to prove the supervisor wrong.

Fifth Session

The therapist began the session by exploring with the family whether there had been any signs of relapse or drug use. William reported with a big smile that he encountered five opportunities to get "high" over the past week, but successfully fought off the peer pressure to use. The therapist shook William's hand and shared with him how he would enjoy laughing at his supervisor. The therapist had William share with the family how he had managed to maintain his sobriety under tremendous peer pressure. William's main coping strategies were to avoid parties and certain peers who abused chemicals, and to spend free time practicing his electric guitar. The family praised William for doing so well.

The mother reported to the therapist that Michele and William were getting along better. In fact, Michele shared with the therapist that she "no longer had the desire" or "felt the temptation" to "take over as the mother around the house." As a vote of confidence, the therapist scheduled the sixth session one month later. The therapist concluded by meeting alone with William. William was praised by the therapist and given the homework assignment of paying close attention to what he does to avoid the temptation to "get high" over the next four weeks.

Sixth Session

One month later, the Smiths came into the office smiling and pleased with the various changes they had made. Mrs. Smith reported that she had not seen any signs of drug use on William's behalf. In fact, she had thought about cancelling the session due to "things going so well." William had secured a part-time job doing stock work in a bookstore.

The therapist explored with the family the various changes they observed in their relationships. Both children shared with the therapist how their mother was a "totally different person," socializing frequently and displaying no signs of being depressed. William pointed out to the therapist that he and Michele were now "good buddies." The therapist explored with the family what they would need to do to "go backwards." Each family member was clearly able to distinguish their old maladaptive ways of interacting from their new dance steps with one another. William read off a list of ten things he did to help resist the temptation to "party" over the past four weeks. After praising William, the therapist asked the family how they would use the therapy session time if no further appointments were scheduled. Mrs. Smith shared with the therapist that she would go to an aerobic class. The children said that they would use their appointment time to be with their friends.

The therapist pointed out to the family that "life is full of ups and downs," and most likely they would run into difficulties down the road. He voiced his confidence in the family's ability to take on new challenges and quickly bounce back to their new positive pattern. The family mutually agreed to terminate therapy. Before leaving the office, William hugged the therapist and thanked him for helping him survive the earlier relapse.

Follow-Up

One year later, the mother reported in a follow-up phone conversation that William had greatly improved in school and continued to remain drug-free. The mother shared with the therapist that she was "addicted" to aerobics.

REFERENCES

Baither, R.C. (1978). Family therapy with adolescent drug abusers: A review. *Journal of Drug Education, 8,* 337-343.

Cleveland, M. (1981). Families and adolescent drug abuse: Structural analysis of children's roles. *Family Process, 20,* 295-304.

Ellis, D.C. (1986). *Growing up stoned.* Pompano Beach, FL: Health Communications.

Fishman, H.C., Stanton, M.D., & Rosman, B.L. (1982). Treating families of adolescent drug abusers. In M.D. Stanton, T.C. Todd & Associates (Eds.), *The family therapy of drug abuse and addiction.* New York: Guilford.

Friedman, A.S., Utada, A., & Morrissey, M.R. (1987). Families of adolescent drug abusers are "rigid": Are these families either "disengaged" or "enmeshed" or both? *Family Process, 26,* 131-148.

Friedman, R.H. (1974). Family system and ecological approach to youthful drug abuse. *Family Therapy, 1,* 63-78.

Haley, J. (1973). *Uncommon therapy.* New York: Norton.

Haley, J. (1980). *Leaving home.* New York: McGraw-Hill.

Hendin, H., Pollinger, A., Ulman, R., & Carr, A.C. (1981). Adolescent marijuana abusers and their families. NIDA Research Monograph, No. 40, 17-25.

Hendin, H., & Pollinger-Hoss, A. (1985). The adaptive significance of chronic marijuana use for adolescents and adults. In J. Brook, D. Lettieri, & D.W. Brook (Eds.), *Alcohol and substance abuse in adolescence.* New York: The Haworth Press.

Howe, B.J. (1974). Family therapy and the treatment of drug abuse problems. *Family Therapy, 1,* 89-98.

Huberty, D.J. (1975). Treating the adolescent drug abuser: A family affair. *Contemporary Drug Problems*, *4*, 179-194.

Joanning, H., Gawinski, B., Morris, J., & Quinn, W. (1986). Organizing a social ecology to treat adolescent drug abuse. *Journal of Strategic and Systemic Therapies*, *5*, 55-66.

Kandel, D.B. (1973). Adolescent marijuana use: Role of parents and peers. *Science*, *181*, 1067-1070.

Kandel, D.B. (1974). Inter- and intragenerational influences on adolescent marijuana use. *Journal of Social Issues*, *30*, 107-135.

Kandel, D.B. (1975). Some comments on the relationship of selected criteria variables to adolescent illicit drug use. In D.J. Lettieri (Ed.), *Predicting adolescent drug abuse: A review of issues, methods, and correlates* (DHEW Publication No. ADM 76-299, National Institute On Drug Abuse). Washington, DC: U.S. Government Printing Office.

Kaufman, E. (1984). Adolescent substance abuse in Anglo-American families. *Journal of Drug Issues*, *14*, 365-377.

Kaufman, E. (1985). Adolescent substance abusers and family therapy. In M.P. Mirkin & S.L. Koman (Eds.), *Handbook of adolescents and family therapy*. New York: Gardner.

LaForte, J., & Todd, T.C. (In press). *Paradoxical prescriptions: The use of written prescriptions in strategic therapy*. New York: Guilford.

Levine, B.L. (1985). Adolescent substance abuse: Toward an integration of family systems and individual adaptation theories. *American Journal of Family Therapy*, *13*, 3-16.

Madanes, C. (1981). *Strategic family therapy*. San Francisco: Jossey-Bass.

Madanes, C. (1984). *Behind the one-way mirror*. San Francisco: Jossey-Bass.

Palazzoli, M. S., Cecchin, G., Prata, G., & Boscolo, L. (1978). *Paradox and counterparadox*. New York: Jason Aronson.

Piercy, F., & Frankel, B. (1985). *Training manual: Purdue brief family therapy*. West Lafayette, IN: Media Based Services.

Piercy, F., & Frankel, B. (1986). Establishing appropriate parental influence in families with a drug abusing adolescent: Direct and indirect methods. *Journal of Strategic & Systemic Therapies*, *5*, 30-39.

Reilly, D.M. (1975). Family factors in the etiology and treatment of youthful drug abuse. *Family Therapy*, *2*, 149-171.

Reilly, D.M. (1984). Family therapy with adolescent drug abusers and their families: Defying gravity and achieving escape velocity. *Journal of Drug Issues*, *14*, 381-391.

Reilly, D. (1979). Drug-abusing families: Intra-familial dynamics and brief triphasic treatment. In E. Kaufman & P. Kaufmann (Eds.), *Family therapy of drug and alcohol abuse*. New York: Gardner Press.

Selekman, M. (1987). Ally or foe? Strategic use of the adolescent substance abuser in family therapy. *Journal of Strategic and Systemic Therapies*, *6*, 12-29.

Simon, R. (1987). Goodbye paradox, hello invariant prescription: An interview with Mara Selvini-Palazzoli. *Family Networker*, *11*, 16-34.

Stanton, M.D. (1979). Family treatment approaches to drug abuse problems: A review. *Family Process*, *18*, 251-280.

Stanton, M.D. (1981). Who should get credit for change which occurs in therapy? In A.S. Gurman (Ed.), *Questions and answers in the practice of family therapy*. New York: Brunner/Mazel.

Stanton, M.D., & Todd, T.C. (1981). Engaging "resistant" families in treatment: II. Principles and techniques in recruitment: III. Factors in success and cost effectiveness. *Family Process*, *20*, 261-293.

Stanton, M.D., & Todd, T.C. (1982). The therapy model. Chapter in M.D. Stanton, T.C. Todd & Associates, *The Family therapy of drug abuse and addiction*. New York: Guilford.

Stanton, M.D., Todd, T.C., Heard, D.B., Kirschner, S., Kleiman, J.I., Mowatt, D.T., Riley, P., Scott, I.M., & Vandeusen, J.M. (1978). Heroin addiction as a family phenomenon: A new conceptual model. *American Journal of Drug and Alcohol Abuse*, *5*, 125-150.

Stanton, M.D., Todd, T.C., & Associates (1982). *The family therapy of drug abuse and addiction*. New York: Guilford.

Szapocznik, J., Kurtines, W.M., Foote, F.H., Perez-Vidal, A., & Hervis, O. (1983). Conjoint versus one-person family therapy: Some evidence for the effectiveness of conducting family therapy through one person with drug-abusing adolescents. *Journal of Consulting and Clinical Psychology*, *51*, 990-899.

Szapocznik, J., Kurtines, W.M., Foote, F.H., Perez-Vidal, A., & Hervis, O. (1986). Conjoint versus one-person family therapy: Further evidence for the effectiveness of conducting family therapy through one person with drug-abusing adolescents. *Journal of Consulting and Clinical Psychology*, *54*, 395-397.

Todd, T.C. (1981). Paradoxical prescription: Applications of consistent paradox using a strategic team. *Journal of Strategic and Systemic Therapies*, *1*, 28-44.

Todd, T.C. (1988). Developmental cycles and substance abuse. Chapter in C. Falikov (Ed.), *Family transitions: Continuity and change over the family life cycle*. New York: Guilford.

Weeks, G.R., & L'Abate, L. (1982). *Paradoxical psychotherapy*. New York: Brunner/Mazel.

Weidman, A.A. (1985). Engaging the families of substance-abusing adolescents in family therapy. *Journal of Substance Abuse Treatment*, *2*, 97-105.

Treating Intrafamilial Child Sexual Abuse from a Systemic Perspective

Sheila C. Ribordy

SUMMARY. This paper examines a systemic approach to a specific form of child sexual abuse, father-daughter incest. While the father is responsible for the sexual abuse per se, a systems approach to incest believes that there are a variety of family dynamics present in incestuous families. These family dynamics center around structural issues (particularly regarding boundaries), problem-solving deficiencies, and dysfunctional communication patterns. Sample family treatment programs are examined. The goals of these programs center around changing family structure, enhancing conflict resolutions skills, and altering family communication patterns. Preliminary treatment outcome data for these family treatment programs is promising.

Child sexual abuse takes many forms from violent rape by a stranger to fondling of the genitals by a girl's own father. All forms of child sexual abuse can have serious negative effects on the abused child, as well as the family as a unit. Because of its prevalence and its strong impact on the family system, father-daughter sexual abuse will be the focus of this review. Sexual abuse involving daughters and their fathers is commonly called incest or intrafamilial child sexual abuse. In this paper, the term, father, will be used to indicate biological father, stepfather, and other father-figures.

Father and daughter incest is the most common form of intrafamilial child sexual abuse (Alter-Reid, Gibbs, Lachenmeyer, Sigal, & Massoth, 1986) and is the most frequently treated by family

---

Sheila C. Ribordy, PhD, Department of Psychology, DePaul University, 2323 North Seminary, Chicago, IL 60614.

therapists (Trepper & Traicoff, 1985). Such sexual abuse can involve fondling of genitals, oral-genital contact, and vaginal or anal penetration. Deliberate exhibitionism and the use of children in the creation of pornographic materials also constitute child sexual abuse. Schechter and Roberge (1976) describe sexual molestation of children as "the involvement of dependent, developmentally immature children and adolescents in sexual activities that they do not fully comprehend, are unable to give informed consent to, and that violate the social taboos of family roles" (p. 129).

EFFECTS OF INCESTUOUS SEXUAL MOLESTATION ON CHILDREN

There has been abundant literature documenting an assortment of effects of child sexual abuse (e.g., Alter-Reid et al., 1986; Boatman, Boatman, & Schetky, 1981; Browne & Finkelhor, 1986; Gold, 1986; Hartman & Burgess, 1986; MacFarlane & Waterman, 1986; Mrazek, 1983; Orzek, 1985; Pelletier & Handy, 1986; Peters, 1976; Swanson & Biaggio, 1985). These are often categorized as short-term and long-term effects.

Short-Term Effects

Common immediate effects of child sexual abuse are self-blame, shame, and guilt. These feelings may result from an egocentric developmental cognitive style common to younger children (Orzek, 1985) or be a reaction to the statements made by the offender regarding the child's role in the sexual behavior. Self-blame, shame, and guilt then become motivations for secrecy. Other incentives for a child's not revealing the abuse are a sense of fear generated through threats made by the offender and a desire to protect family members and to keep the family intact (Burgess, 1986; Swanson & Biaggio, 1985).

Other short-term effects of child sexual abuse include appetite problems, nightmares and sleeping problems, enuresis, social disinterest and isolation, phobias and fears regarding going to school or leaving the house, somatic complaints, running away, self-destructive behavior and suicidal tendencies, sexual acting-out and excessive masturbation, general oppositional and acting-out behaviors, impaired ability to trust, repressed anger and hostility, pseudomaturity, failure to achieve age-appropriate developmental tasks, depression, and substance abuse.

Long-Term Effects

Besharov (1978) has referred to child sexual abuse as a "psychological time bomb." He suggests that the symptoms may not be immediately obvious and only over time will the real magnitude of the effects be seen. While some of the short-term symptoms abate over time, many others persist well into adulthood (Russell, 1986). As seen from some of the studies of adults who were sexually abused as children, there are also additional effects that plague one's adulthood. The literature has described the following as long-term effects of child sexual abuse: lowered self-esteem—both general and sexual, guilt and self-blame, sexual fears and dysfunction, chronic depression, self-destructive behaviors, substance abuse, confused identity, psychosis, interpersonal difficulties—especially related to intimacy and trust, and somatic complaints.

A final long-term characteristic to be discussed here is the sense of powerlessness and helplessness that is reported by victims long after the abuse has ceased. This "learned helplessness" and the victimization experience may well leave sexual abuse victims passive and susceptible to later-life victimization and abuse such as rape, marital rape and spouse battering (Besharov, 1978; Steele & Alexander, 1981).

Mediating Factors

A number of researchers and clinicians have reported on mediating factors which can exacerbate the negative effects of child sexual abuse (Friedrich, Urquiza, & Beilke, 1986; Hoier, 1987; Orzek, 1985; Pelletier & Handy, 1986). In sum, this literature suggests that effects are likely to be worse if the abuser is known to the victim, if force and serious threat are used, if the age difference is large between the victim and the offender, if the type of abuse is more severe and intrusive, and if the abuse lasts over a longer period of time. Friedrich et al. (1986) found that when sexual abuse was initiated in early childhood, an internalizing pattern of symptoms was manifested, while older children tended to externalize. A similar pattern was found for sex of the victim, with girls tending to internalize more than did boys.

CHARACTERISTICS OF THE INCESTUOUS FAMILY

Systemic theorists focus on the structure of the family when looking at any distinguishing characteristics of incestuous families. These structure-based issues have centered around boundaries, roles, and communication patterns (Sgroi, 1982; Trepper & Traicoff, 1985).

One of the most pervasive family characteristics that is cited in the incest literature is that of confused and blurred boundaries. This can occur between the family and the environment where the family is often isolated from extrafamilial contact and influences (Alexander, 1985), among family members as a whole in which enmeshment and cross-generational boundary violations are characteristic (Larson & Maddock, 1986), or within dyads in the family. The three most frequently discussed dyads are the father-daughter dyad, the parental dyad, and the mother-daughter dyad.

Father-Daughter Dyad

Larson and Maddock (1986) have characterized four father-daughter incestuous relationships. The first, *affection-exchange*, involves a misguided attempt to show and receive affection in an atmosphere in which there is a perceived deprivation of love and attention. The second form, *erotic-exchange*, involves early socialization of the child to family values regarding free sexual play and open eroticism within the family. Individual privacy is not allowed, and there are strong, yet subtle, forces in effect which require compliance with the family norms. Both of these first two types of incestuous relationships rarely involve overt threat or violence.

The third type of incestuous relationship, *aggression-exchange*, involves the expression of hostility and anger through the scapegoating of a vulnerable member of the family. The father's actions often are related to frustrations and stresses, and his behavior is impulsive and angry. *Rage expression* is the fourth incestuous relationship type. This relationship is also marked by hostility and violence; however, the perpetrator is not reacting to frustrations and stresses but to an "existential rage" which is often based in a childhood history of abuse and neglect. Both of these latter two forms typically include other family violence as well as the incest (i.e., spouse battering, physical child abuse), and the fathers are characterized by significant individual psychopathology.

Of these four types, family treatment including father is indicated in the first two forms. Affection-based incest is easiest to work with and involves families who have the greatest strengths to bring to treatment. Goals typically center around strengthening the couple relationship of the parents and helping family members express affection in more appropriate ways. A very directive form of family therapy is required with the erotic-based incest family. Strongly held beliefs need to be challenged, and initial treatment goals focus on reeducation and on changing attitudes. Once attitudes have been altered, these enmeshed families need to establish appropriate boundaries honoring individual privacy and the family hierarchy, and they need to find alternative ways of sharing affection.

For the incestuous families in which hostility and violence are common, family therapy without the father is usually indicated. Father might be included later, but only after significant progress in dealing with his own individual psychopathology and when the safety of family members can be assured. Family treatment with the remaining family members centers on their roles as victims by empowering them and reestablishing intrafamilial relationships based on mutual support and nurturance. As the fathers rarely are reintegrated into these families, mothers need to be bolstered for their roles as single parents and heads of house.

Husband-Wife Dyad

Stern and Meyer (1980) have outlined three types of couple patterns in father-daughter incest families: (1) possessive-passive, (2) dependent, inadequate man-strong, domineering woman, and (3) dependent-dependent. The first type, possessive-passive, refers to a domineering husband who controls his passive wife and his children. The family is clearly a patriarchy with very traditional sex roles, and the husband may use force and intimidation to manipulate and control the family (Herman, 1981; Swanson & Biaggio, 1985). Part of the father's control comes through keeping the wife and children relatively isolated from extrafamilial resources (Alexander, 1985). The wife in such a family is described as dependent, passive, powerless, and inadequate. In reviewing published case histories involving father-daughter incest, this seems to be the most common couple configuration reported.

The second type – dependent, inadequate man-strong, domineering woman – is characterized by a strong wife who is more motherly than wifely to her husband. She is said to be cold and perhaps rejecting of the children, and is perceived to be emotionally and physically unavailable by the children and her husband. The dependent, inadequate father often resorts to alcohol or drugs to generate feelings of power and forcefulness. His sexual dominance over a child may also meet this need. The dependent-dependent couple consists of two parents who are both largely inadequate in meeting both their spousal and parental obligations. Such families are often multi-problemed and chaotic in structure, leaving a feeling that no one is in charge. The parents often turn to the children for emotional support and nurturance. In general, the incest literature rather uniformly describes parental conflicts and difficulties as common in the incestuous family (Giaretto, 1982; Pelletier & Handy, 1986; Swanson & Biaggio, 1985). These couple conflicts cover most areas of the marital and parental relationship.

Mother-Daughter Dyad

The mother-daughter dyad has also received much attention in the literature. The most common dynamic attributed to this dyad is role-reversal – a situation in which the child (usually the eldest daughter) assumes many of the responsibilities of the mother (Pelletier & Handy, 1986). This may occur because of psychological inadequacies of the mother, physical disabilities, an over-worked and tired mother (many children and few resources), or a frequently absent mother. The daughter gradually takes on the tasks of caring for siblings, doing housework, and being emotionally supportive of the father. It is assumed then that it is not such a large step for the father to look to the daughter for his sexual needs as well. Carter, Papper, Silverstein, and Walters (1986) suggest that girls may hesitate to approach their mothers about the incest, because they see the mothers as inadequate and powerless within the family structure.

In the literature describing the family dynamics of incestuous families (most of which is based on clinical experience), mothers often receive more attention and criticism than do abusive fathers themselves (Herman, 1981; Machotka, Pittman, & Flomenhaft, 1967). In fact, there have been recent criticisms of what is perceived to be a weakness of systemic approaches to conceptualization and treatment of incest families (Carter et al., 1986; Conte, 1986; Finkelhor, 1986). In an effort to deal with the whole family as a system, a family perspective may diminish the role of the father and the actual sexual abuse (Conte, 1986), as well as unduly put responsibility for family dynamics and the occurrence of the abuse on the mother (Carter et al., 1986; McIntyre, 1981; Wattenberg, 1985). These could be legitimate concerns. Yet, as will be evidenced from the treatment approaches that are described later in this paper, it is possible to recognize and work with existing family dynamics while also underscoring the seriousness of the abusive behavior and the father's responsibility for it. The important distinction is between holding a mother responsible for someone else's sexual abuse of her daughter and her normal responsibility to parent and protect her daughter once the abuse is disclosed. At that point, the mother's role may be quite critical to the continued safety of her daughter. Thus, effective systemic approaches have a primary treatment goal of empowering the mother and strengthening her role in the family.

Communication Patterns

Besides structural variables in the incestuous family, Alexander (1985) has also emphasized dysfunctional communication patterns. She refers to these families as "closed systems," because they have minimal information exchanges with their environment. Family members are family-focused and regard the environment as threatening. Because of inadequate communication within the family as well as minimal interchange with the environment, incestuous families are rigid in their problem-solving skills. There is an inability to flexibly accommodate to developmental changes as well as external stresses. In such an enmeshed system, any attempts at independence are met with pressures for conformity and loyalty. Thus, family secrets are left unchallenged. Alexander also suggests that because these families easily become threatened by change, there is too much homeostasis in operation. Under threat they will present a united front to maintain the status quo (Larson & Maddock, 1986). While normal families also have a tendency to remain the same, they balance this with a need to evolve over time. Incestuous families, however, are overly governed by the need to maintain stability and predictability. Such family dynamics make it unlikely the abuse will be disclosed without outside support (Swanson & Biaggio, 1985).

Before leaving the topic of characteristics of incestuous families, it is important to point out that the family dynamics outlined above are primarily based on clinical experiences and case histories. While this is a legitimate source of knowledge, it is important that controlled investigations be undertaken before assuming this set of dynamics is standard for incestuous families. Even if such dynamics were commonplace, it is inaccurate to assume that certain family dynamics cause child sexual abuse. These dynamics may just as well result from or be secondary to the abuse. Additionally, as Finkelhor (1986) accurately points out, conceptualizations of these family dynamics have come primarily from father-daughter incest, and cannot be assumed to generalize to father-son, mother-son, mother-daughter, or extrafamilial child sexual abuse. Until such time as we can be more confident of our speculations, it is important to conduct careful and thorough assessments of each incestuous family that presents for treatment.

SYSTEMIC TREATMENT OF INCEST

Mrazek (1983) reports that there have been four ways of treating child sexual abuse: (1) the perpetrator is treated for the sexually deviant behavior (individual, group), (2) the victim is treated for trauma (individual, group), (3) the family is treated for its dysfunctioning system, and (4) a combination of the above. No matter which of the treatment approaches taken, there seems to be universal agreement that an important role of the therapist is to do case management and coordination with the variety of agencies and authorities that become involved in such cases (Anderson & Shafer, 1979; Giaretto, 1982; Mayer, 1985). Because these families can easily manipulate service providers and legal authorities against one another, it is important that a united and coordinated effort be used to deal with the family. Contrary to that reported in much of the rest of the psychotherapy literature, clinicians working with incest families feel it valuable to have legal and criminal authorities involved in "forcing" treatment (Anderson & Shafer, 1979; Boatman et al., 1981; MacFarlane & Bulkley, 1982). Sex offenders are difficult to get in voluntary treatment, and incest families often present a united front in their resistance to treatment once they have recovered from the shock of disclosure. Child protection workers and juvenile and criminal authorities can act as the authority in pushing a family into treatment, which leaves the therapist to serve more of an advocacy role for the family. Nevertheless, work with incest families requires a therapist to be relatively directive and limit-setting, while still being empathetic and supportive. "Respect for clients is essential but needs to be tempered by an awareness of their ability to manipulate and project blame" (Anderson & Shafer, 1979, p. 443).

A systemic treatment approach recognizes that all family members are affected by the sexual abuse, and that they each can play a role in restructuring the family and preventing further abuse. Involving the family in treatment also allows for more thorough monitoring of ongoing abuse, allows the therapist to utilize less resistant members to eventually engage those who are more reluctant to become involved in treatment, and allows the therapist to treat the problem behavior within its context. MacFarlane and Bulkley (1982) point out that the goal of family treatment is not necessarily to keep the family intact, even though it is widely recognized that in father-daughter incest there is often a strong desire on the part of the family (and an ambivalence on the part of the daughter) to remain together as a family (Solin, 1986; Trepper & Traicoff, 1985). While family treatment often begins with family members being separated by father's removal or the child's placement outside the family, a family's cooperation in treatment can lead to eventual family reunification.

Family treatment programs are often multi-faceted in character, using other treatment modalities in conjunction with family treatment (Anderson & Shafer, 1979; Barrett, Sykes, & Byrnes, 1986; Giaretto, 1982; Giaretto, Giaretto, & Sgroi, 1978; Trepper & Traicoff, 1985). There is often a thorough diagnostic phase which allows for a careful assessment of individual family members, significant dyads, and the family as a whole with emphasis on the dynamics and processes outlined earlier in this paper (Boatman et al, 1981; Sgroi, 1982). In addition to interviews and psychological testing, indirect means like play therapy can be used to gather assessment information. The assessment information is then used to determine how and when family therapy is indicated. In the case of very sociopathic and/or violent fathers, family therapy may not be the treatment of choice (Larson & Maddock, 1986). Also, it may be indicated that family sessions are not appropriate until a later point in treatment (Alexander, 1985). For instance, if a daughter has been traumatized badly, individual therapy may be warranted for her before she faces her family, especially her father (Swan, 1985). Also, if the mother is undecided about whether she wants to work at saving her marriage, then father's inclusion in family therapy sessions may be premature. The initial assessment may also have pointed out special problems such as alcoholism which may need to receive specific treatment before family work can progress. Individual therapy, couple therapy, group therapy, and self-help group experiences (i.e., Alcoholics Anonymous, Parents United) have been widely used as adjuncts to family therapy (Giaretto, 1982; Finkelhor, 1986; Larson & Maddock, 1986).

The goals of family therapy with incestuous families usually include the following:

1. Stopping any further occurrence of the child sexual abuse and any violence that may also be going on in the family.
2. Father's acceptance of responsibility for the sexual abuse.
3. Mother's acceptance of responsibility for protecting the children.
4. Empowering the mother and the victim.

5. Strengthening the marital relationship (this usually requires couple therapy, parent training and/or specific sexual dysfunction counseling).
6. Clarifying the roles of family members such that these roles are age-appropriate and do not violate generational boundaries.
7. Strengthening the mother-daughter relationship.
8. Improving family communication patterns.
9. Clarifying or establishing healthy family rules.
10. Helping the family build problem-solving and conflict resolution skills.
11. Helping the family to develop appropriate means of nurturing and sharing affection.
12. Supporting differentiation and autonomy of individual members.
13. Encouraging the family's development of extrafamilial relationships and the reduction of social isolation.

James and Nasjleti (1983) suggest that family therapy with incestuous families requires special deviations from traditional family therapy. It may be necessary to have longer family sessions than is usual, or to have the flexibility of continuing until an agenda is completed. They also recommend, as do many others, that a co-therapy team be utilized, and a male-female team is preferable. Sessions may need to be held in places other than the therapist's office. For instance, home visits or meeting at a site at which the child victim feels safest may be indicated. Clear agendas for each session need to be established and strictly adhered to during the session. And finally, James and Nasjleti feel the therapist should be flexible but also assertive, directive and controlling of the process.

SAMPLES OF STRUCTURAL-STRATEGIC
FAMILY THERAPY PROGRAMS

Two comprehensive family therapy approaches based on a structural-strategic model are reviewed below (Barrett et al., 1986; Trepper & Traicoff, 1985). These two programs were selected for description here as they seem representative of the general literature on the systemic treatment of incest (Anderson & Shafer, 1979; Giaretto, 1982; Giaretto et al., 1978; James & Nasjleti, 1983).

Trepper and Traicoff (1985) characterize their approach to the treatment of incestual families as structural-strategic. They utilize a thorough assessment phase often lasting a month or more which involves seeing the parents alone for the initial session, psychological testing for mother, father, and the abused child(ren), and a second session involving all family members in which the incest may or may not be discussed (this is left up to the family at this point). This family session is primarily diagnostic in nature, with the authors organizing their conception of the family around Olson's Circumplex Model (Olson, Sprenkle, & Russell, 1979). Thus, cohesion, adaptability, and communication patterns are examined. The lengthy assessment phase is used to determine whether family therapy is appropriate. If a family continues in treatment, specific family and individual goals are established using a Goal Attainment Scaling system.

The initial phase of family treatment is concentrated on the couple. Weekly couple sessions are held in order to prepare the parents for the "Apology Session" (Trepper, 1986). The goal of the apology session is to have father and mother face the children and acknowledge each's responsibility for the child sexual abuse and family situation. Concurrently, there may be individual sessions with the victim daughter to prepare her for the apology session as well. The apology session itself is ritualized so that the parents sit united facing the children. Each has rehearsed (in the previous couple sessions) what he/she will say. The entire family is present, and the apology session may be videotaped for later use in family therapy. Trepper sees the apology session symbolizing the new desired structure for the family with the parents being united, there being clear generational boundaries, and the parents are assuming responsibility for the nurturance and safety of their children. The therapist's role in this session is to coach the parents in their presentations and to encourage the children to ask questions. Finally, particular attention is paid to the victim's willingness to accept the apology (this does not mean that she is required to give up her anger), and if she does accept the apology, to emphasize that from this point forward, the goals of treatment will be to build a new family structure that will ensure future safety for all the children. There is particular concern that the daughter not use the past abuse in a manipulative way in the future. Trepper's use of the apology session provides a good example of family therapy's not de-emphasizing the responsibility of the father, and it seems to address the criticisms of systemic treatment that were discussed earlier.

While Trepper and Traicoff (1985) feel occasional individual treatment of father or daughter is necessary, their primary emphasis is on couple and family therapy. Insight, modeling, behavioral, paradoxical/strategic and restructuring techniques are all utilized in the family treatment which typically lasts 1 1/2 to 2 years. Termination is gradually introduced, with sessions faded out over time. Using this treatment model, Trepper and Traicoff report a recidivism rate of 4% after treatment of more than 50 families.

Barrett et al. (1986) also describe a structural-strategic family therapy program for intrafamilial child sexual abuse. The goals of treatment consist of changing the structure of the family, improving communication, and reducing and/or eliminating dysfunctional behavioral patterns. Using Schwartz et al.'s (1984) assessment and stage model, they envision family treatment in three phases: (1) Creating a context for change, (2) Challenging patterns and expanding alternatives, and (3) Consolidation. During the first phase, a primary role of the therapist is to coordinate services and provide case management, especially while legal decisions are being made and placement is being considered. Individual sessions might be necessary with specific family members to deal with denial. These individual sessions are used along with family treatment. Both assessment and treatment concentrate on family structure. Individual and family assessments are regarded as critical, and extended family members may also be included in assessment and/or treatment. In this initial phase, the issue of responsibility is dealt with overtly, and both individual and family treatment goals are specified.

In the second treatment phase, emphasis is on restructuring. Couple sessions and family sessions are used to establish clear boundaries, reduce rigidity or chaos, develop conflict resolution skills and enhance communication abilities. Supplementary group sessions that deal with chemical abuse, family violence, or sexual abuse can be excellent adjuncts to the family treatment at this stage. The final phase is characterized by the family being given increased responsibility to solve their own problems. Sessions are spaced out and potential future problems are discussed. Total treatment typically lasts 1 to 1 1/2 years. After working with more than 250 families with this model, the authors report a recidivism rate of only 2%.

THERAPIST ISSUES

Issues which are critical in work with incestuous families involve the therapist's own thoughts, feelings, and reactions. There are many indications in the incest literature that countertransference is an especially important issue when working with incestuous families (Boatman et al., 1981; Giaretto et al., 1978; Swanson & Biaggio, 1985). Some common troublesome reactions experienced by therapists who have worked with child sexual abuse include: (1) over-identification with the victim, (2) feelings of anger and blame toward the father (and perhaps the mother), (3) feelings of powerlessness and fatigue, (4) avoidance of or embarrassment regarding sexual material, and (5) anxiety and lack of confidence.

When a therapist overly identifies with the victim, there is danger that rescuing behavior will be present (Giaretto et al., 1978). Victim dependency may be promoted (Swanson & Biaggio, 1985), and the therapist may not be open to hearing the stories of other family members (and thus, miss parts of the whole picture and fail to connect with other members).

Anger at the father usually manifests as excessive blaming of the father or encouraging family members' anger toward the father even when it interferes with family therapy progress. While the therapist does not need to like the father, the therapist needs to want to help the father. Often it is easier to keep the anger in perspective if the father can also be seen as a victim (perhaps of his own childhood), or if some of the father's feelings of contrition, embarrassment, loneliness, self-hate, etc. can be acknowledged as underlying the inevitable defensiveness with which fathers first present themselves. Giaretto et al. (1978) report that having weekly staff meetings, in which therapists are encouraged to ventilate and resolve negative feelings, have been very helpful.

Therapists' feelings of powerlessness and fatigue usually come from having unrealistic expectations of what can be accomplished (especially since these are often multi-problemed families) and from doing too much of the work that the family should be doing for itself. The therapist may have an agenda he/she is trying to accomplish with which the family has not agreed to cooperate. Fatigue is also a common manifestation of working with very emotionally draining material. Working as a co-therapy team is one of the ways to avoid burnout. Others are to have regular supervision or consultation in which the countertransference issues can be examined. Finally, it is important that the child sexual abuse therapist be able to detach oneself from his/her work when appropriate. Having healthy outlets for tension and rewarding activities and relationships in one's personal life are important anecdotes to burnout.

Any therapist who is going to work with incestuous families needs to feel comfortable listening to and discussing sexual matters (Berliner & Stevens, 1982; Swanson & Biaggio, 1985). Furthermore, the therapist often needs to educate members of the family about sexual issues, and thus, should also be very knowledgeable about the entire area of sexuality — sexual development, sexual orientation, sexual dysfunction, physiology, contraception, etc. Utilizing a male-female co-therapy team can make discussion of sexual issues easier, but is no substitute for a therapist's achieving comfort with the topic on his/her own.

Anxiety and lack of confidence are symptoms of a therapist who is either ill-trained and/or ill-prepared to work with the special problems of incestuous families. Beginning therapists and therapists who have not worked with such families, will require preparatory education and close supervision as they work on their initial cases. Work with incestuous families requires a therapist style which is directive and limit-setting, as well as supportive and empathetic. Some therapists may be excellent at being supportive but have a difficult time taking charge and being confrontive with clients.

Such therapists are not likely to be effective with incestuous families.

CONCLUSIONS

This paper reviewed the literature which has taken a systemic view of father-daughter incest. A systems approach to father-daughter incest views the child abuse as occurring within specific family dynamics. While the father must be held responsible for the sexual abuse per se, it is believed that there are a number of structural, problem-solving, and communication deficiencies in incest families. Consequently, systemic treatment programs emphasize changing family structure, bolstering conflict resolution skills, and changing communication patterns. It is rare, however, that family therapy would be offered as the sole treatment modality. Couple, individual, and group sessions are often used as part of the family therapy. The family therapist who treats incest families will find it necessary to emphasize case management as well as family therapy, because of the legal and social agencies who are involved.

There is now preliminary evidence of the effectiveness of family treatment for father-daughter incest which utilizes a structural-strategic model. While the issues are complex in incest cases, family structure and dynamics can be altered through family therapy so that the recurrence of the incestuous behavior is minimized.

REFERENCES

Alexander, P. (1985) A systems theory conceptualization of incest. *Family Process, 24,* 79-88.

Alter-Reid, K., Gibbs, M. S., Lachenmeyer, J. R., Sigal, J. & Massoth, N. A. (1986) Sexual abuse of children: A review of the empirical findings. *Clinical Psychology Review, 6,* 249-266.

Anderson, L. M. & Shafer, G. (1979) The character-disordered family: A community treatment model for family sexual abuse. *American Journal of Orthopsychiatry, 49,* 436-445.

Barrett, M. J., Sykes, C., & Byrnes, W. (1986) A systemic model for the treatment of intrafamily child sexual abuse. *Journal of Psychotherapy and the Family, 2,* 67-82.

Berliner, L. & Stevens, D. (1982) Clinical issues in child sexual abuse. *Social Work and Child Sexual Abuse, 1,* 93-108.

Besharov, D. J. (1978) Child sexual abuse: Incest, assault, and sexual exploitation. A special report from the National Center on Child Abuse and Neglect. DHEW Publication No. (OHDS) 79-30166.

Boatman, B., Boatman, E. L., & Schetky, D. H. (1981) Treatment of child victims of incest. *The American Journal of Family Therapy*, *9*, 43-51.

Browne, A. & Finkelhor, D. (1986) Initial and long-term effects: A review of the research. In Finkelhor (Ed.) *A sourcebook on child sexual abuse*. Beverly Hills, CA: Sage Publications.

Burgess, A. W. (1986) *The sexual victimization of adolescents*. National Center for the Prevention and Control of Rape. Rockville, MD: NIMH.

Carter, B., Papper, P., Silverstein, O., & Walters, M. (1986) The Procrustean bed. *Family Process*, *25*, 301-304.

Conte, J. R. (1986) Sexual abuse and the family: A critical analysis. *Journal of Psychotherapy and the Family*, *2*, 113-126.

Finkelhor, D. (1986) Sexual abuse: Beyond the family systems approach. *Journal of Psychotherapy and the Family*, *2*, 53-65.

Friedrich, W. N., Urquiza, A. J., & Beilke, R. L. (1986) Behavior problems in sexually abused young children. *Journal of Pediatric Psychology*, *11*, 47-57.

Giaretto, H. (1982) A comprehensive child sexual abuse treatment program. *Child Abuse and Neglect*, *6*, 263-278.

Giaretto, H., Giaretto, A., & Sgroi, S. M. (1978) Coordinated community treatment of incest. In Burgess, Groth, Holmstrom & Sgroi (Eds.) *Sexual assault of children and adolescents*. Lexington, MA: Lexington Books, 231-240.

Gold, E. (1986) Long-term effects of sexual victimization in childhood: An attributional approach. *Journal of Consulting and Clinical Psychology*, *54*, 471-475.

Hartman, C. R. & Burgess, A. W. (1986) Child sexual abuse: Generic roots of the victim experience. *Journal of Psychotherapy and the Family*, *2*, 83-92.

Herman, J. L. (1981) *Father-daughter incest*. Cambridge, MA: Harvard University Press.

Hoier, T. S. (1987) Child sexual abuse: Clinical interventions and new directions. *Journal of Child and Adolescent Psychotherapy*, *4*, 179-185.

James, B. & Nasjleti, M. (1983) *Treating sexually abused children and their families*. Palo Alto, CA: Consulting Psychologists Press.

Larson, N. R. & Maddock, J. W. (1986) Structural and functional variables in incest family systems: Implications for assessment and treatment. *Journal of Psychotherapy and the Family*, *2*, 27-43.

MacFarlane, K. & Bulkley, J. (1982) Treating child sexual abuse: An overview of current program models. *Social Work and Child Sexual Abuse*, *1*, 69-91.

MacFarlane, K. & Waterman, J. (1986) *Sexual abuse of young children*. New York: Guilford Press.

Machotka, P., Pittman, F. S., & Flomenhaft, K. (1967) Incest as a family affair. *Family Process*, *6*, 98-116.

Mayer, A. (1985) *Sexual abuse: Causes, consequences, and treatment of incestuous and pedophilic acts*. Holmes Beach, FL: Learning Publications.

McIntyre, K. (1981) Role of mothers in father-daughter incest: A feminist analysis. *Social Work*, November, 462-466.

Mrazek, P. J. (1983) Sexual abuse of children. In B. Lahey & A. Kazdin (Eds.) *Advances in clinical child psychology, Vol 6*. New York: Plenum Press, 199-215.

Olson, D. H., Sprenkle, D. H., & Russell, C. S. (1979) Circumplex model of marital and family systems I: Cohesion and adaptability dimensions, family types, and clinical applications. *Family Process, 18*, 3-28.

Orzek, A. M. (1985) The child's cognitive processing of sexual abuse. *Journal of Child and Adolescent Psychotherapy, 2*, 110-114.

Pelletier, G. & Handy, L. C. (1986) Family dysfunction and the psychological impact of child sexual abuse. *American Journal of Psychiatry, 31*, 407-412.

Peters, J. J. (1976) Children who are victims of sexual assault and the psychology of offenders. *American Journal of Psychotherapy, 30*, 407-408.

Russell, D. E. H. (1986) *The secret trauma: Incest in the lives of girls and women*. New York: Basic Books.

Schechter, M. D. & Roberge, L. (1976) Sexual exploitation. In Helfer & Kempe (Eds.) *Child abuse and neglect: The family and the community*. Cambridge, MA: Ballinger.

Sgroi, S. M. (1982) Family treatment of child sexual abuse. *Social Work and Child Sexual Abuse, 1*, 109-128.

Solin, C. A. (1986) Displacement of affect in families following incest disclosure. *American Journal of Orthopsychiatry, 56*, 570-576.

Steele, B. F. & Alexander, H. (1981) Long-term effects of sexual abuse in childhood. In Mrazek & Kempe (Eds.) *Sexually abused children and their families*. New York: Pergamon, 223-234.

Stern, M. J. & Meyer, L. C. (1980) Family and couple interactional patterns in cases of father/daughter incest. In Jones, Jenstrom, & MacFarlane (Eds.) *Sexual abuse of children: Selected readings*. Washington, DC: U.S. Government Printing Office.

Swan, R. W. (1985) The child as active participant in sexual abuse. *Clinical Social Work Journal, 13*, 62-77.

Swanson, L. & Biaggio, M. K. (1985) Therapeutic perspectives on father-daughter incest. *The American Journal of Psychiatry, 142*, 667-674.

Trepper, T. S. (1986) The apology session. *Journal of Psychotherapy and the Family, 2*, 93-101.

Trepper, T. S. & Traicoff, M. E. (1985) Treatment of intrafamily sexuality: Conceptual rationale and model for family therapy. *Journal of Sex Education and Therapy, 11*, 18-23.

Wattenberg, E. (1985) In a different light: A feminist perspective on the role of mothers in father-daughter incest. *Child Welfare, 64*, 203-211.

The Systemic Treatment of Bulimia

Richard C. Schwartz
Pam Grace

The compulsive bingeing and purging of food, a syndrome that has come to be known as bulimia, has received increasing interest from clinicians and researchers since the relatively recent discovery earlier in this decade of its remarkable prevalence, primarily among women. Because this syndrome is clearly impacted by several different levels of system, e.g., the socio-cultural level, the family level, and the individual intrapsychic level, it can and has been understood and treated very differently depending on which level theorists or clinicians have focused.

For the most part, models for treating bulimia have emphasized one of these levels while devoting far less attention to the other levels, so treatment approaches have been relatively narrow, and limited. This is because theorists have lacked a model that allows one to shift fluidly across levels, using the same principles at each level. This paper presents a model that allows theorists and clinicians to shift from one of these levels to another, as needed, because it views all these levels of system as operating according to similar principles and as highly interconnected.

Some models emphasize the impact of the socio-cultural level, e.g., the pressure on women to be thin, the subordinate status of women, the cultural tendency to look to food for comfort, etc., and work at helping bulimics reexamine their values and behavior in light of these issues (e.g., Boskind-White and White, 1983). Ther-

---

Richard C. Schwartz, PhD, is Coordinator of Training and Research, Institute for Juvenile Research, 907 S. Wolcott, Chicago, IL 60612.

Pam Grace, MA, is a doctoral candidate, Department of Psychology, University of Illinois, Chicago.

89

apy derived from these models usually brings clients together into groups to discuss these issues and support each other in trying to change.

Other theorist/clinicians, relying on their clinical impressions and interviews with families, have focused on the interactional patterns of the families of bulimics that are thought to maintain the syndrome. Schwartz, Barrett and Saba (1984) reported that many bulimic families resemble the "psychosomatic families" described by Minuchin, Rosman and Baker (1978), in that they often demonstrated the characteristics of enmeshment, over-protectiveness, rigidity and lack of conflict resolution. In addition, they found these families to be highly isolated, conscious of appearances, and attributed special meaning to food and eating. Root, Fallon, and Friedrich, (1986) categorized bulimic families as either perfectionistic, overprotective, or chaotic, depending on such variables as how the family handled conflict and child rearing. Both of these groups of theorists advocated that the treatment of the bulimic include significant others whose active involvement they believed is crucial to positive outcome.

The most common approach to treating bulimics, however, has focused on some aspect of the individual client's struggle with herself. Most of the work in this area has come from the cognitive-behavioral school which attempts to change both the behaviors and irrational cognitions that surround the binge/purge episode, whether in group or individual therapy (Fairburn, 1984).

As is apparent in the review above, the first author was part of this montage of disconnected approaches by emphasizing the importance of family factors over the other two levels. This changed, however, when, out of his frustration with the limitations of working exclusively with the bulimic's external context, he began to explore with some clients their internal life and how it also was maintaining of this syndrome (Schwartz, 1987a). From those explorations he developed a model that extends systemic thinking into the realm of internal process. With this model, called the Internal Family Systems model, it is possible to see the similarities between the interactions within an individual's "external" family and their "internal" family. It is also possible to intervene at either level using the same systemic paradigm and techniques, rather than having to shift from a systemic at the family level, to, for example, a psycho-dynamic or cognitive/behavioral paradigm at the internal level.

In addition, the same paradigm has proven useful for appreciating the impact of the socio-cultural context on the families and individuals embedded within it (Schwartz, 1988). For example, the degree to which a culture, in evaluating its members, emphasizes the importance of material success and vogue appearance over personal qualities such as the ability to be direct or nurturant, will be the degree to which aspects of families and individuals will demonstrate isomorphic imbalances. Unless we can understand the connections between our society's imbalances and those within the families and clients we treat, we will not be able to help them reexamine which socio-cultural values are best for their family or themselves.

UNDERSTANDING THE BULIMIC SYSTEM

While the entire model cannot be described in this space, we will focus on some aspects of it as they apply to families and individuals that have been highly influenced by and strive to achieve the predominant middle class values of the United States, a group that we call "hyper-Americanized," and that we found constituted about one-third to one-half of the families in our study (Schwartz et al., 1984). We will begin by describing the parallels between such a hyper-Americanized bulimic client's internal life and the values of her family.

The Bulimic's Internal System

If a bulimic client is asked to describe her internal experience that surrounds a binge/purge episode, she is likely to describe experiencing a cacophony of inner "voices" or conflicting thought patterns and emotions for a period preceding the binge, during which time she feels increasing tension. The binge itself often quiets or distracts from this internal distress as she feels as if she has become an unthinking, unfeeling "eating machine." As the awareness of the calories being consumed increasingly sinks in, however, another kind of tension mounts which only the purge can diminish.

If asked to focus on the nature of each of these internal voices, many bulimics can identify and differentiate a variety of what can be considered subpersonalities or "parts" of them, each of which has a different intention, view of the world, and strategy for influencing her. In addition, if asked certain questions, a client usually can describe how she relates to each of these parts of her—i.e., how she likes it and it likes her, how often it is around, how often she listens to it and does what it wants—and how the parts relate to each other. When one part comes to dominate the internal process or becomes suppressed or dominated, then symptoms occur. When suppressed parts are expressed, they appear in extreme form. Similarly, rapid fluctuation of high conflict between parts can also render "symptoms." From this kind of interviewing it is possible to get a picture of this internal group as an interacting system in much the same way one gets a picture of a family by tracking relationships and interaction patterns.

That many aspects of a bulimic client's internal system seem to parallel aspects of her external family is not surprising because we believe that the prominent values and themes of her family will determine which parts of her she likes and listens to and which she does not. For example, a bulimic raised in a hyper-Americanized home, will often overvalue and listen to an "achievement part" that pushes her to compete and do perfect work and a dominating "approval part" that tells her she must look perfect to attract a man because she has little else to offer. In addition, she will reject or try to avoid the angry parts of her or the parts that want intimacy and are sad and lonely, because her family, dominated by themes of proper appearance or competitiveness, also disdains these "weaknesses."

Such a strong, controlled exterior is difficult to constantly maintain, particularly since her angry or sad parts are extreme from lack of attention, and these parts will periodically "take over" much to her embarrassment and guilt. These displays of "unsavory" feelings will also bring disdain or over-reaction from her family which will compound her guilt and determination to push these parts away. The more she tries to eliminate these parts the more they struggle to take over. To avoid having this internal struggle go on indefinitely an "indulgent" part will activate and make her think only of eating, thereby distracting her from the internal turmoil, and the binge/purge cycle is under way. Thus, the bulimia can serve as a distraction from internal conflict in much the same way as it can distract her family from the conflicts resulting from their overvaluing of achievement and appearances and undervaluing assertiveness and intimacy.

With this model then, a therapist will have the same goals whether working at the individual or the family level with these hyper-Americanized bulimic families. At the individual level the goal is to help her control and be less identified with her extremely critical achievement and approval parts while accepting and acting on the nonextreme desires of neglected parts like intimacy and anger. In so doing she increasingly will be able to control and change the role of the indulgent part that triggers the bingeing because its distracting or nurturing role will be less necessary.

At the family level, the goal is similarly to help all members of the family become less obsessed with achievement and appearances so that they can face and deal assertively with the issues that divide them. This allows family members to define their relationships directly rather than indirectly negotiating relationships through who is eating what and how much.

The Hyper-Americanized Family

We have found that the hyper-Americanized families that surround some bulimic clients tend to place extreme importance on appearing stylishly attractive and inordinately successful at all times, and at any cost. These values are reflected in a constant pressure to dress fashionably, to get good grades, to make or marry into a lot of money, and to look "healthy and attractive" (which means look thin). The self absorption and scrutiny as well as the competitiveness that accompanies these values contributes to a family attitude that people should be able to control themselves and should be strong, because the world will take advantage of any weakness.

Relatedly, these families believe that they must at least appear to be perfect, and perfect families do not have conflicts, addictions, or depressions. As in the internal life of the hyper-Americanized bulimic client, this pressure to be strong and perfect cannot always prevent overt conflicts from surfacing or sadness from showing. When one or more members display such a "lack of self control" they do so in an extreme way in part because everyone is so afraid of such episodes and reacts so strongly to them. Such outbreaks are followed by attempts to minimize or deny the episode so as to maintain the perfect image or by harsh sanctions against the family member who is seen as precipitating it. It is difficult to exist in such a family without some kind of distraction or method of self-numbing, and it is common to find heavy use of alcohol or tranquilizers in the parents and drug abuse in siblings, in addition to strange eating practices in all members.

In keeping with being highly Americanized, these families are often extremely male-oriented in the sense that men are viewed as more important and valuable than women and so the best chance for a woman to advance is to attract a successful man. Women in these families learn early that the approval of men in general, and their father in particular, is of primary importance, which often leads to competitive feelings among them for his approval. Often the client protects her father from her mother's angry outbursts and feels that she has a special, yet precarious, relationship to him. In some cases it is the sudden loss of this special closeness, often during the sexually charged adolescent period, and the ensuing sense of emptiness, confusion and disapproval that precipitates the bulimia. Often fathers in these families have been overt in their preference for thin, attractive women so the client's approval part is further activated.

Daughters in these families come to see their female peers as competitors and male peers as potential mates and, consequently, have few real friends. Thus their lives are spent in a lonely search for a man to take care of them. They feel great when they get even slight romantic attention from an attractive man or, relatedly, when they have lost weight as a step toward getting such attention, and terrible if they do not get or if they lose such attention, or gain weight.

In addition, these daughters are given conflicting mandates from their families regarding what their life goals should be. Consistent with the perfect family image and competitive approach, they are pushed to achieve in school in an area that the parents value, and yet are to be nice, and nonthreatening (nonassertive and nonintellectual), so as to attract "Mr. Right." Thus their achievements are inconsistently praised and attended to which reflects their family's ambivalence regarding female achievement. The parents' inconsistent praise for success and consistent criticism for imperfection becomes a model for the way the client's achievement part treats her.

Finally, for many of the reasons outlined above, these hyper-Americanized family systems are not very fulfilling contexts in which to live. Caught up with their extreme achievement parts, fathers work long hours and are preoccupied when they are home. Mothers are often lonely but feel lucky to be married to such successful men and so are afraid to express this loneliness because they do not want to further burden their husbands, who tend to recoil from their unhappiness.

Mothers in such predicaments are likely to become highly involved in their daughters' lives. Many of the bulimic clients we see find themselves in the role of their mother's confidant, therapist or companion. They are trying to comfort and cheer up their mother more often than vice versa, and are usually unsuccessful because they cannot change her context. Clients often report feeling a mixture of guilt and frustration due to mother's unhappiness, and resentment that she was/is so preoccupied as to not be more of a mother to them. Mothers feel a similar mixture of concern over the client's health and frustration with her irresponsibility and inability to control herself—to better model the perfect child. This mixture of extreme feelings (or parts) in the mother-daughter relationship is usually quite combustible and fights erupt quickly over petty issues like eating, dressing, or cleaning. Such fights are more bitter when the client is also protective of her father or in competition with mother for his approval. When her parents are unhappy with each other, the client's parts are highly activated in a complex and confusing inner cacophony that often precedes a binge.

Why Bulimia?

In light of these values and issues, the client's selection of food as a primary indulgence becomes more understandable. Food is the arch enemy of her achievement and approval parts since, in their eyes, eating leads to weight gain which ultimately leads to rejection by men. Thus, binge eating is seen by those parts as evidence that she is a gluttonous, weak-willed failure. The other parts, such as angry or rebellious parts, that are in opposition to and generally dominated by the achievement and approval parts, then would encourage her to binge eat in defiance of that dominant diet-obsession.

In addition, because members of these families are often so preoccupied with their own personal dramas and are uncomfortable with expressions of sadness, a pattern develops of parents trying to cheer up distressed children by giving them food rather than by comforting them directly. Thus a child learns to look for comestible instead of personal consolation when hurt. Food will fill one up and will not reject one or expect anything in return. Thus the binge satisfies several parts at once — angry or rebellious parts that do so out of defiance, sad or lonely parts that do so looking for nurturance, and, as mentioned above, protective parts that do so to provide a distraction from the internal turmoil. In addition, thinking of oneself as "a bulimic" can reassure those protective parts that fear failure by ensuring that one will not try anything truly risky, like getting close to someone or leaving one's parents' home, until one is no longer "a bulimic."

At the family level, the client's bulimia reassures the parts of her parents that fear life without her, by showing that she is a long way from growing up and still needs their help. It also can provide a "safe" conflict between family members over how best to handle her problem. Finally, it can provide an excuse for the client's displays of anger, depression or other imperfections.

It is important to note however that, in some cases, the bulimic client's symptoms do not appear to serve any indirectly protective function within her family, such as those mentioned above. In addition, even where there appears to be evidence that the syndrome is embedded in indirectly protective sequences, it is a mistake to assume that family members desire or have a stake in the maintenance of the syndrome. Rather, it should be understood that everyone feels oppressed by her symptoms but, sometimes, the family will use bulimia in a distractive or protective way without being aware that such use maintains or exacerbates the syndrome. In other cases, the bulimia itself will generate difficult sequences in the family that ultimately result in a need for a distraction.

TREATING THE BULIMIC SYSTEM

We have portrayed bulimia as a syndrome embedded in both internal and external sequences of interaction that activate each other. That is, the way a bulimic client's hyper-Americanized family relates to her will activate certain sequences among her internal parts that will, in turn, make her behave in ways that activate extreme sequences among family members, and so on. For change in such systems to be lasting, both the internal and external systems need to be reorganized to some degree. Fortunately, we have found that changes at either level affect parallel changes at the other level, so it is possible, for example, to focus only on family interactions and simultaneously change the client's internal system, and vice versa.

With this perspective, the job of the therapist, initially, becomes to assess which level of system (internal or external) is most amenable to change and, later, to shift the focus of therapy back and forth from internal to external as indicated by the reaction of the bi-level system. For example, where a client is financially and emotionally dependent upon and living with her hyper-Americanized family, working exclusively with her internal system is likely to result in only temporary improvement at best. This is because (1) the external sequences she is amid every day are likely to be so activating of extreme parts that she will not have room to do much internal work, and (2) if she were to rapidly improve and become more independent her untreated family is likely to react in ways that undermine these changes, because of their mixed feelings regarding her independence.

Thus, unless a bulimic client has plenty of room to change, it is wise initially to focus on helping the family explore and change interaction patterns that activate her internal parts and, in that way, contribute to her bulimia. In this process the therapist can lead the family in a reexamination of their values, their living context, and how those factors contribute to the client's problem. To do this without generating defensiveness the therapist needs to adopt the attitude of a researcher who is trying to collaborate with the family in coming to a better understanding of their predicament. If the therapist is successful in maintaining such an attitude, it will be possible to create with the family an understanding of therapy as a vehicle for all family members to work together. The shared purpose can be to find ways to help each family member, but particularly the client, control or calm down the internal parts of them that are interfering in their lives.

Therapeutic Questions

We have found the following sets of questions yield useful discussions in this endeavor. As the therapist and family explore the above questions, and continually relate them to the client's bulimia, the patterns that activate the client's parts will emerge and can be addressed, again, in a cooperative effort with the family. It is important the discussion be related, not by giving an interpretation but by sincerely asking the family for any connections that they can make. The therapist may pose each question he or she believes applicable to the family in general or, instead, ask who in the family most embodies the values related to the question.

I. Family's Reaction to Bulimia

Many aspects of a family's system of values are revealed in how they have reacted and are currently reacting to the client's symptoms. Often simply discussing these attempted solutions, and the degree to which they are effective, will generate new reactions that will give the client more room to change.

1. How have different family members reacted to and tried to handle the client's bulimia? Who most often tries, or is most likely to try, to ignore or deny symptoms? Who is most likely to try to coerce, intimidate or scorn the client into stopping? Does any family member protect the client from another member or from the outside world because of the bulimia? What are other approaches that have been attempted by family members and what interaction sequences tend to surround the syndrome now? How do these various approaches or sequences

affect the client's internal parts that are involved with the bulimia?

2. How do family members view the client, particularly as related to the bulimia (e.g., as weak, rebellious, a victim, sick, or selfish)? How do these beliefs affect what internal parts tell the client about her/himself? How do family values affect their views of the client (e.g., feelings toward weakness or lack of self-control or inability to control the client). How do different views of the problem contribute to inconsistent or contradictory approaches to it, and the interaction sequences they generate?

3. How does their focus on or concern about the bulimia affect each family member's life? What would happen if the client did not have this problem (e.g., who might be able to do things or talk about issues or talk to each other in ways that they cannot now)? How does the client's awareness of this role of the syndrome affect the internal parts?

4. What might a family context look like that would support the client's efforts to control or calm down the parts involved in bulimia sequences? What parts or values or family members might interfere with the creation of such a context? How could those members be helped to control those parts of them?

The goal of this series of questions is to help the family see that they all (including the client) have internal parts that, when activated by the syndrome, generate interaction patterns that are related to the maintenance of it. With that new view, they can begin to work together to keep those parts of them all from interfering in their lives.

II. Current Family Context

The lasting success of the family's efforts to change their reaction to the client's symptoms will depend on several other factors that can also be explored with the family and are illustrated in the following questions.

1. How physically and emotionally isolated is the family as a unit and is each member; i.e., how much access does each member have to a supportive network and is that satisfactory? Do they have particular values that tend to increase this isolation (e.g., competitiveness, fear of extrafamilial, self-sacrifice)? How does this isolation from outsiders affect the way they relate to each other and to the client?

2. How accessible are they to each other? Who nurtures whom and how? Who is too busy to be supportive or supported? Do they have values that maintain this intrafamily isolation? How does this intrafamily isolation affect the way they relate to each other and to the client?

3. Are there current stresses on key family members that are contributing to patterns of isolation and conflict (e.g., life stage crises, job stress, dealing with a chronic or acute illness, or a loss of an important relationship)?

4. How happy are key members with their current living situation as it relates to their isolation and to the activation of extreme values like hyper-concern with appearances and achievement, or the over-valuing of males?

5. Who in the family does the client worry about the most? How does the client try to help or protect those people? Is this protection necessary and are there other, more direct, ways to help the family? How do these worries affect the client's internal parts? How do the values and isolation of the family contribute to the degree to which these worries are warranted?

The goal of this series of questions is to orient the family to an awareness of how these issues of isolation, stress and emotional support are related to the degree to which they will be able to successfully reorganize their relationships to the client such that work on the internal system can proceed.

III. Family Values

The following are values or beliefs that we have encountered in these hyper-Americanized families that we believe contribute to the elements of context for bulimia outline above. The therapist can ask the family members about the degree to which they subscribe to the following values, and how those might contribute to the clients problem.

Women should:

1. be competitively achieving in areas that are attractive to high achieving men, but should not threaten men.
2. look perfectly vogue so as to attract a high achieving man.
3. be able to control themselves. Fat is a sign of indulgence and weakness and unhappiness or anger is a sign of lack of gratitude or appreciation for her position in life.
4. expect to be taken care of by a man materially but not necessarily emotionally.
5. see other women as rivals for men, who should not be trusted.
6. have a perfectly clean house, perfectly behaved kids, successful husband, etc.
7. be careful because men will take sexual advantage of them at any opportunity. They need to be protected from temptation.

Members of their family are:

1. to be thought of and given priority before one thinks of oneself.
2. the only ones to rely or depend on. Outsiders are out to get you.
3. basically very close and nice. One can always find things to complain about but it is better to think positively and not dwell on problems.
4. special, better than most people, and should prove that in their achievements and appearance.

Parts Language

Throughout the discussions generated by the questions outlined above we find it helpful to lead the family in using what could be called "parts language" when describing any extreme feelings or values, e.g., "so a part of you believes that a woman is only as valuable as the man she lands, but other parts do not agree" or "so you have a powerful achievement part that never gives you a break—do you like that?" One of the most useful aspects of the "parts" frame for understanding bulimia is that family members and the client are more able to admit and commit to work on behaviors that contribute to the problem when those behaviors and thoughts are seen as only small parts of them than when they are seen as aspects of their core personality. Thus the parts language helps create an atmosphere of nondefensive exploration that is an unusual and welcome experience for these families.

In addition, the therapist is lifted out of the position of having to try to control the client's bulimia directly or coerce the family into changing the way they treat her. Instead, all members of the therapist/family system are united in collaboration to find a way to keep their extreme parts from running and ruining their lives. During this process the therapist may begin to work individually with the client on changing her relationships with parts of her that are involved in the bulimic sequences and gradually increase the time devoted to that individual work as her family gives her more room to do that work. Specific elements of this kind of individual work have been described elsewhere and so will not be repeated here (Schwartz, 1987a, 1987b).

CASE EXAMPLE

Sara Smith was an attractive 17-year-old high school junior, an only child, living with her parents. The Smiths were an attractive, personable and articulate family who epitomized the hyper-Americanized family described previously. They came to therapy because Sara's binge/purge cycle was disrupting their otherwise peaceful existence.

Mr. Smith could not understand why Sara couldn't just control herself. He was a great proponent of self discipline and felt very uncomfortable showing vulnerability or being in the presence of those who did. His attitude inculcated in Sara an achievement part that disdained her own weak and vulnerable parts. Similarly, Sara's mother tried to keep a "stiff upper lip" but frequently fell victim to bouts of despair or rage. Because Mr. Smith hated weakness, Mrs. Smith was unable to turn to him for emotional support, and consequently Sara became very concerned about and reactive to her mother's depression. Heated battles between mother and daughter erupted when her mother was upset, and the focus of these fights was Sara's eating.

As in the hyper-Americanized family pattern described previously, Sara's family was highly male-oriented. Both Sara and her mother valued her father above themselves and competed with each other for his approval. Sara was desperate to keep the approval of her father. Thus her achievement and approval parts became extreme and highly influential. Being thin was a frequent focus of both of these parts because Sara's father (like all other men, she believed) liked his women that way.

This family system created a context for the kind of polarized parts that are commonly found in the internal sequences of bulimics. These included (1) a part that worried about her parents' welfare and told her to be sacrificial, rather than selfish, (2) a part that wanted her to achieve and became highly critical if she did not listen to it or if she acted sad or weak, (3) a part that wanted her to look perfect and which became highly critical of her eating habits, (4) a part that became extremely sad, lonely and helpless since she received little nurturance from her parents, and (5) a part that told her to indulge or that took over and made her binge.

By asking her about these parts and their dialogues in various situations, a symptom-maintaining sequence among them became evident. For example, her father might say something to her about her poor school performance and this slight would activate the achievement part to berate her for being so lazy and worthless. That criticism always stirred up the sad part that would make her feel hopelessly depressed, and at times, suicidal. To protect her from these scary feelings, the indulgent part took over at that point and she would binge. During the binge however, the appearances part reminded her of all the weight she could be gaining and made her vomit. After the episode, the achievement part again began to berate her, this time for being so gluttonous and undisciplined — and that berating would trigger the sequence to repeat, sometimes three or four times a day.

Because Sara was living at home, it seemed appropriate to begin in therapy by addressing issues within the family system first, and then work on her internal family system later in the course of therapy. The initial focus at the family level was on Sara's relationship with her mother. During sessions, Sara and her mother were encouraged to talk more directly with one another while the father was prevented from interrupting. As the therapist raised questions regarding the way that their family viewed men and women or achievement, and the impact of these views on them, Sara and her mother began to confront their competitive feelings for Mr. Smith's attention, which was difficult but necessary for the improvement of their relationship. In order to facilitate their focus on these issues, a moratorium was declared on the parents' attempts to get Sara to stop bingeing because as long as they were actively fighting over that battle ground, they could avoid these more difficult issues. Gradually, mother and daughter came to see that they could enjoy each other's company.

As his wife's and daughter's relationship improved and they began to do things together, Mr. Smith, who was used to being the center of attention, became increasingly demanding. When his wife and daughter did not revert to competing for his attention, he too had to become more direct in stating his needs. For the first time, he told Sara directly how important it was to him to have his "little girl" near him. And Sara was able to tell him that she could no longer be his little girl and needed to have a life for herself. Such directness laid the groundwork for a more appropriate type of relationship; one in which Sara had the freedom to be the young adult that she was becoming.

Changes in the Smith family affected Sara's internal family system as well. The work with her mother had deactivated the part that worried about her mother's depression since she saw that her mother was strong enough to deal with difficult issues and seemed happier in doing so. The part of Sara that was so concerned with the approval of men, especially her father, also became less dominating and extreme; she came to see her father in a less perfect, more human way. Through this period, her bulimia waxed and waned but no longer was the central focus of her existence.

Individual sessions revealed that while a number of Sara's more extreme parts had calmed down the sequence remained (although less intense). Now her sad parts became less extreme because her critical parts (which told her to reject or ignore the sad part) were less active. Still the indulgent part was activated when Sara became sad, and thus her bingeing continued. In therapy Sara was encouraged to listen to the sad part, acknowledge its pain, and learn to comfort it. Soon that part became less needy and with Sara's continued attention to it, she experienced less sadness. The indulgent part took over much less often and found a new role in advising her about when and how to have fun, and Sara's bingeing greatly reduced.

After several months of this kind of work with her parts, while simultaneously working with her parents in marital therapy, Sara not only stopped bingeing and purging but also began to eat when she was physiologically hungry rather than emotionally hungry. This is considered an important sign of change because it means that her parts have calmed and are allowing her to experience and trust natural body sensations. Therapy ended after approximately one year. Sara had stopped the bulimic behavior altogether. She is presently enrolled in a college in a neighboring state and appears to be enjoying it and doing well.

REFERENCES

Boskind-White, M. and White, W. (1983). *Bulimarexia: The binge/purge cycle.* New York: Norton.

Fairburn, C. G. (1984). Bulimia: Its epidemiology and management. In A. J. Stunkard and E. Steller (Eds.), *Eating and its disorders.* New York: Rowan Press.

Minuchin, S., Rosman, B. and Baker, L. (1978). *Psychosomatic families: Anorexia nervosa in context.* Cambridge: Harvard University Press.

Root, M., Fallon, P., and Friedrich, W. (1986). *Bulimia: A systems approach to treatment.* New York: Norton.

Schwartz, R. (1987a). Working with "internal and external" families in treatment of bulimia. *Family Relations,* 36, 242-245.

Schwartz, R. (1987b). Our multiple selves. *Family Therapy Networkers,* 11, 24-31, 80-83.

Schwartz, R. Problems as symptoms of a lack of fit among a family's structure, values and context, manuscript in progress.

Schwartz, R., Barrett, M. and Saba, G. (1984). Family therapy for bulimia. In D. Garner and P. Garfinkel (Eds.), *The handbook for the psychotherapy of anorexia nervosa and bulimia.* New York: Guilford Press.

The Family School System:
The Critical Focus
for Structural/Strategic Therapy
with School Behavior Problems

Dennis E. McGuire
Elina R. Manghi
Patrick H. Tolan

SUMMARY. It is argued that a focus on the home-school system is critical in working from a Structural/Strategic approach to child school problems. The Structural/ Strategic conception of these types of problems is presented with a focus on three areas of difference between home and school subsystems that are likely generators of problems: beliefs, structure, and developmental adaptation. Techniques for assessment and intervention are presented.

Approximately 25% of students evidence some form of school problems. School problems are one of the three most common reasons for referral to mental health practitioners (Tolan, Ryan, & Jaffe, 1988; Viale-Val, Rosenthal, Curtiss, & Marohn, 1984). Within this general referral category several more specific problems can be identified including disruptive behavior, low motivation, truancy, and behavioral problems related to learning disabilities. These statistics and array of manifestations indicate it is a serious and apparently recalcitrant problem.

Dennis E. McGuire, ACSW, is affiliated with the Institute for Juvenile Research, Chicago, IL. Elina R. Manghi, LP, is affiliated with Catholic Charities, Chicago, IL. Patrick H. Tolan, PhD, is affiliated with DePaul University.

Correspondence should be addressed to Dennis E. McGuire at the Institute for Juvenile Research, 907 S. Wolcott Ave., Chicago, IL 60612.

For the present purposes a school behavior problem is defined as any behavior which is considered disruptive of normal learning, classroom functions, or activities by the child, teacher, and/or parents (Kessler, 1966; Eno, 1985). Problems manifest at school may or may not manifest at home (McGuire & Lyons, 1985). Also, problem level may range in severity from mild disturbance such as periodic disruptive behavior or failure to complete some schoolwork, to more severe problems such as truancy or delinquent behavior. Behavior problems may precede and interfere with learning. Likewise, underachievers and learning disabled children may develop behavior problems as a derivative of their academic difficulties. Although it is important to distinguish between academic achievement problems such as learning disabilities and school conduct problems such as disciplinary problems and between problems that are due more to the setting such as poor schools or low employee interest than individual student differences, children and families having these problems share many similarities and are at-risk for the same poor outcomes (Kessler & Albee, 1975). In addition, realistic intervention for most of these problems include the same components. Therefore, we argue they can be approached with the same general framework by a family therapist. In each case, the problem and ensuing intervention need to be conceived and implemented as a home-school system problem.

FAMILY AND SCHOOL CHARACTERISTICS RELATED TO SCHOOL PROBLEMS

There is a massive literature on the determinants of school success and school problems and multiple facets of school adjustment have been studied (Coleman, 1966; Rutter, 1983). Rather than survey that material or discuss specific factors' comparative importance, for the present purpose it is only necessary to identify two aspects of the literature that are most pertinent for family therapists. First, it appears that family attitudes and behaviors about school are the salient family contributors to success or problems (Rutter, 1983). For example, Scheinfeld (1983) found that achieving children come from families that emphasize the values of motivation, exploration, and engagement with the world, while the families of non-achieving children emphasize constraint, isolation and control of the world. Similarly, Garbarino (1982) concludes the child's school success is attributable to the "academic culture" of the home, which refers to the extent to which the family fosters and models appropriate learning and social skills, values education, and supports the particular school and teacher. We contend familial attitudes are expressed through interaction around school related family activities such as homework.

On the other hand, school influences seem to occur as environmental constraints that exacerbate or foster negative familial attitudes. For example, teacher bias and negative expectations can impede achievement significantly (Brophy & Evertson, 1981; Good, 1980).

The second pertinent aspect that can be culled from the literature is that the family and school characteristics' effects interact in their influence (Johnson, 1980). Johnson (1980) identified aspects in each of these two spheres most conducive to learning. They are the family values and expectations for learning and the school factors of the teacher's skill and personality style. Further, we suggest as has been implied by others, home and school not only interactively determine the child's behavior, but their influence is as interdependent components of a system (Minuchin, Biber, Shapiro, & Zimiles, 1969). For example an adolescent boy's interest in auto mechanics rather than academic coursework may generate substantial conflict with his parents but only become a problem if the school promotes his involvement in this interest. Or, a family problem, such as an alcoholic parent, may absorb a child in worry thereby inhibiting school performance.

Most family treatment models of school problems acknowledge that the problem results from the interaction of the home, school, and child. Nonetheless, for the most part, the actual interventions implemented tend to view the influences as independent and focus on one area as primary; i.e., the child (Baker, 1979; Gutkin, 1981), the home (Atkeson & Forman, 1979), or the school (Caplan, 1970). This type of conceptualization assumes that one "component" is the genetic locus of the problem and that change in one area will generalize to the secondary influences. However, none of the singular focus approaches have consistently produced impressive outcomes (McGuire & Lyons, 1985). For example, the assumption that changes brought about by an intervention in the family system alone will generalize to the child's school performance have been demonstrated for behavioral disruptions but without accompanying change in academic achievement (Santa-Barbara, Woodward, Levin, Goodman, Streiner, & Epstein, 1979). Similarly, change in school behavior may not generalize to home or be maintained without additional "family therapy" (McGuire & Cimmarusti, 1986; McGuire & Lyons, 1985).

Over the past ten years a promising new family systems approach to school problems has developed which expands the "system" to emphasize the interaction of the home and school in determining child behavior. Family systems therapists have traditionally focused on the patterns of interaction in a family is problem solving which serve to maintain problems. This family focused approach, however, needs to be expanded to focus on how school personnel, family members, and the child interact around the school problem. From this view, each of the different spheres, although independent systems in many ways, in regard to a child's school problems are interdependent system components (family, school, child). They are one system because of their convergent impact on the child's academic functioning. They must be understood in total to intervene effectively. This approach is the basis of the interventions suggested in this paper.

Family therapists may be inclined to dismiss this difference as negligible or reject it because it moves the intra-familial interaction from primacy as the reason for the problem and the focus of the intervention. Others may view this approach as counter to a common family therapy view that child school problems are best understood as distractors/regulators of parental marital problems. Regardless of the extent to which problems exist or are most evident in a specific system, the therapist must not ignore the interaction between all of the systems in evaluating the problem and in designing intervention. This shift to conceiving of the home-school interaction as systemic may appear to require a simple incorporation of school personnel as consultants to the family therapy. Actually, it represents a shift for family therapists analagous to that required by the conceptual shift from the focus on individual characteristics to family interactions. The components or subsystems need to be understood through their systemic functions, not as separate concerns. Described by Aponte (1976) as "intervening where the systems touch together," this overall system can be labeled the home-school system.

The home-school view provides several advantages in formulating solutions. For example, it allows the therapist to address the process of interaction of major influences, rather than trying to discern chronological order of the appearance of problems and other aspects of discovering "primacy." Also, it removes blame assignment (diagnosis) from its usual primary position in intervention design and replaces it with the goal of constructing collaborative responsibilities. Focusing only on families requires, implicitly or explicitly, that the therapist ignore school influence or render a judgement that the school's influence on the problem is negligible or negative (e.g., this is not really a school problem or help parents to accommodate to a problematic school). Moreover, failing to consider the home-school system can leave the therapist without sufficient data or leverage to intervene to realize needed change. For example, a pattern of escalating crisis can develop when the school calls the parents to complain about the child's behavior. The parents will pressure the child, which in turn results in more misbehavior by the child, which leads to more serious or more frequent calls from school and so on. This spiraling pattern can not be redirected if the intervention focuses on only one setting. Apparently "effective" interventions will have only limited or temporary effects.

Several views of focusing on home-school system have been put forth. In an early paper, Aponte (1976) demonstrated the impact on the child of home and school together was as important as either separately. Lusterman (1985) suggested the home-school focus provides a structured mediation that counters the pattern of unproductive or overactive interchanges between home and school. McGuire and Lyons (1985) suggested such an approach breaks the cycle of blame between home and school that stagnates the system. They utilized family-school personnel meetings as a way to intervene around conflicts about supervision of homework and re-organize the home-school system. This approach increased homework completion 67% in 17 underachievers' school performance following the meeting and implementation of monitoring.

THE STRUCTURAL/STRATEGIC CONCEPTION OF SCHOOL PROBLEMS

The Structural/Strategic approach to home-school interventions involves using techniques of Structural (Minuchin & Fishman, 1981) and Strategic (Haley, 1976) therapy. It attributes school problems to inconsistency in the role demands made on a child at home and school, his/her behavior must be inconsistent about academic achievement, and school problems will develop. However, it is not just the child who has inconsistent demands. The parents will have conflicting demands in supporting the child in his/her struggle while supporting a pro-school attitude. The teacher(s) will have conflicting demands in wanting to help and understand the child while seeing such attention as disruptive to teaching the whole class.

The Structural/Strategic model is a competency based approach which assumes that people have resources which are not used in their settings (Minuchin & Fishman, 1985). Therefore, the process of intervening with school problems is to sensitively challenge current beliefs and modify interaction patterns by promoting the child's competent academic behaviors. The primary vehicle for accomplishing these tasks is to assess the subsystems (home, school, child, other) and home-school system and frame the problem as a home-school problem that requires joint cooperative effort to monitor the child's completion of academic work. This is usually done over 6-20 sessions focused around setting up and following a family-school meeting. Within the meeting the shared task serves to modify structure, belief, or development conflicts between home and school that are seen as maintaining the problem. The crucial role of inconsistency in systemic functions (roles) across subsystems can be understood as arising from three sources: beliefs, structure, and developmental transitions.

SYSTEMIC SOURCES OF HOME-SCHOOL PROBLEMS

Beliefs are the views members of a family or school have of their roles, responsibilities and constraints and their relations with others in their immediate subsystem. For example, parents may have expectations about involvement in school activities that conflict with expectations of the school. One parent may expect to have weekly school contact with the child's teacher to help direct the child's education while another parent may assume education is the teacher's professional province and therefore only visit the school once a year. School professionals often expect the same extent of parental involvement for all parents which may conflict with parental expectations and lead to labeling of parents as either too intrusive or lacking concern about school.

System structure refers to the organization of the home-school system, and its relation to adjacent subsystems. The most prominent component of structure is the extent and type of boundaries between different subsystems. Boundaries can be understood as the "barriers" determining proximity and hierarchy between system members or across subsystems (Wood, 1985). In the present concern, this would be the availability and type of contact between permitted members of the home-school system. A balance of closeness and distance must exist between system members to ensure both an adequate separation of subsystem functions and yet maintain the cohesion necessary to sustain the component collaborations. In addition, a delicate balance between assuring availability yet maintaining distinct provinces of expertise between parents and teacher(s) is critical. Often rigid impervious boundaries are developed because a workable flexibility cannot be established. For example, a couple may be too absorbed in an intense marital dispute to carry out appropriate monitoring of a child's school work. It is likely a teacher's advice would be viewed as being too proximate to the marital subsystem and placing the teacher above the parents hierarchically on how to manage the child at home. A similar problem, but with reverse hierarchical positions occurs when parents try to direct teachers about how to manage their child in the classroom. As these examples indicate, the proximity and hierarchical aspect of boundaries can be critical to the development of a school behavior problem. A home-school system view promotes adequate consideration of each.

Developmental stages refer to the transformation of systemic roles, goals, and concerns at different points in the life stage (McCubbin & Dahl, 1985). Life span development theory is predicated on the observation that families move through a predictable order of concerns and style of organization at a relatively consistent rate. In addition to family development, individual stages of each generation are occurring simultaneously. For example, while one generation is facing the issues of old age, another one is facing the issues related to the entrance of young children into the school system and the third is facing the issue of leaving infancy. There is a complex process involved in making the transition from phase to phase requiring changes in boundaries and the beliefs of family members. Family stress is usually highest at the transitional stages, so this is when symptoms are most likely to appear (Carter & McGoldrick, 1988; Combrinck-Graham, 1985). For example, a family has to adapt to the change in roles and needs of all family members when children enter into school years. Similarly a school may not be aware of developmentally-driven diminishing interest in school by parents who are getting older and moving to the post-parental stage. The transformations of family development are multifaceted and imply general change in the very organization of the family not just in school issues. Several reviews of the general patterns of such development are available elsewhere (Liddle, 1983). Pertinent to the present concern is that the effects are often expressed as school problems.

Closer examination of specific problems in beliefs, structure, and developmental crises that arise in the family-school system provides a reasoning for intervening at this level.

Belief System Problem

A shared belief of most parents and teachers is that their goal (of a functional home-school system) is to supply complimentary effort, resources, and time to educate the child. What may be less agreed upon is the roles of all system members. This goal of educating involves an integration of a wide range of beliefs, which are expressed as system member interests. The interests of teachers as educational professionals are served through aiding the child's initiative to learn, explore, and adapt in the academic arena. Similarly, the parents have interest in their child's self-satisfaction and well-being that follow from achievement and adaptation. The child has an interest in developing competencies and accomplishments for self-satisfaction as well as pleasing parents and teachers.

In most cases an integration or balance is struck between the subsystems' belief driven interests which ensures the success of education. In other cases however, school behavior problems may result when one or several systems, because of conflicting beliefs, either cannot or will not cooperate in this overall home-school educational goal. For example, a child with an attention deficit disorder, a neurologically based inability to maintain attention, may have limited ability to learn and cooperate with the classroom average methods and activities. A teacher that has a belief that this is willful may severely impede the child's learning by placing inappropriate demands, making erroneous assumptions about motivations, and not providing needed structure in the child's classroom activities. Further, the teacher may feel unable to adequately direct or contain the behavior, disrupting the expected cooperation between child and teacher around the educative tasks. In turn, the family may be blamed for not adequately training their child. If the family believes that education is the sole responsibility of the school, they may not respond to the child's needs or the school's communications adequately. They may assume the teacher has poor skills or a "personality problem." Subsequently, the child's problems will increase.

Thus, the difference in beliefs can lead to school problems. Several common types of home-school differences in beliefs can be identified. School involvement, especially extracurricular activities interfere or compete with family activities and priorities such as work, caretaking, or intimacy functions. Similarly in the home-school interchange, differences in degree of emphasis on educational achievement and, insistence on extrinsic versus intrinsic motivation in academic learning can promote home-school alienation. Differences of socioeconomic class or cultural values and corresponding differences in beliefs about learning and about the family may prohibit cooperation around the educational goal (Falicov & Karrer, 1980).

A well-functioning home-school system often involves a subtle integration of a wide range of interests and beliefs. Successful therapy requires careful consideration of beliefs and interests of each system component.

Structural Problems

Functional home-school systems maintain appropriate organizational hierarchies and boundaries between each subsystem's domain. Specific to the present concern, this involves who sets the rules of behavior management at home and at school (hierarchy) and separation of subsystem functions in the implementation of behavior management (boundaries). Hierarchy and boundary difficulties occur when conflicts exist about responsibilities and control within either the home or school or between the two settings. For example, in families a common type of boundary problem is when marital conflicts spill over to conflicts about behavior management of the child. The inconsistency at the interface of child-parent subsystems can lead to child behavior problems because of split loyalty to conflicting parents (Tolan, Cromwell, & Brasswell, 1986). This can affect the child's school achievement and behavioral compliance in several ways. The child may misbehave in school as an attempt to master the family conflict by replicating it in the school. The child may be absorbed in worry over the possible dissolution of the family which results in poor performance and either withdrawn or disruptive school behavior. Similarly, extensive parental disagreements and related self-absorption may keep the parents from setting up the space and time for the child to complete the homework or properly supervising its completion. The child with unprepared homework is high risk for distraction and disruption in the class (McGuire & Commarrusti, 1986). An older child may be called upon to perform a large portion of the parenting for a taxed, single parent with detrimental effects on his or her school work, which may eventually lead to disruptiveness or truancy (McGuire & Tolan, 1988). Thus, the boundary issues at home can impact strongly on school.

The child's school problem may also be a manifestation of an overly rigid boundary between the family and the school subsystem related to differences of class or culture (as discussed above in beliefs). This rigid boundary may lead to a lack of cooperation at several subsystem levels. These families may have no quiet place or time set aside in the home for study. They may not consider monitoring the child's homework as their responsibility. At the interface between home and school, these families can seem unskilled at negotiating with the school system. Thus, they tend to avoid contact with the school, overreact to school meetings with inappropriate expressions of hurt or anger, or pit the child needlessly against the school (McGuire & Lyons, 1985).

Another boundary rigidity problem is when the school defines certain members of the neighborhood as low in academic interest, and unable to learn. They make little or no attempt to work with anyone from the neighborhood. Finally, parent behavior management style may simply be incongruent with the teacher(s) management style leading to attributions by each that the management style of the other is the cause of the problem and overinvolvement (cross-boundaries) in the other's domain. For example the child from a family with a laissez-faire style may feel it appropriate to move around the class and talk at will. The opposite may also be true. An open classroom may be difficult for the child from an authoritarian family, possibly leading to the child's withdrawal or truancy.

Boundary and hierarchy problems may also manifest because of behavioral management inconsistencies within the school setting itself. For example, a school principal may inadvertently undermine the teacher's efforts to help the child, by regularly suspending the child to try to stop tardiness. The child's absence plus the punishing relationship undermine the academic help provided. Similarly a personal conflict between two school professionals, may come to focus as conflict about managing a given child's behavior.

Developmental Problems

School behavior problems and other family symptoms may signal difficulties the family is having around developmental transitions. For example, the entrance of their children into the school is usually a stressful transition for a family because of the need to adapt to widening social spheres, shift in parental roles and responsibilities, new demands on the child outside the family, and confrontation of differences in the family's beliefs and those of the school or other parents. To return to an example used earlier, the child who is absorbed with the responsibilities and accompanying worry about an alcoholic parent may have difficulty focusing in an age appropriate manner on peers and school responsibilities. In another situation a school phobia may arise in an older sibling when the youngest sibling enters school. By staying at home, the phobic child can maintain vigilance over a depressed parent, make that parent needed, and prevent the family from having to negotiate the impending developmental changes.

Carter and McGoldrick (1988) have distinguished stressors associated with family life stage transitions between those due to the transition into a new life stage and stressors from the family structure and their sustained belief system over time (generations). The former includes developmental or maturational crises as well as life events such as chronic illness, accidents, and external events such as war or economic change which affect status. The latter type act as influences on how transitions are supposed to be managed. Both need consideration in evaluating transition impact. Family transitions can also be affected by other parameters such as socioeconomic status, ethnicity, family size, gender role issues, and losses through death, divorce or remarriage.

In addition to the family's life cycle transitions, therapists need to consider individual developmental issues such as the child's maturational stage which will affect the way a problem is conceptualized and the possible solutions. For example, a developmentally young child may be unable to organize homework assignments without the help of an adult whereas an adolescent may be able to organize the activity but has trouble choosing between seeing friends or participating in extra-curricular activities and necessary solitary homework (Combrinck-Graham, 1985).

IMPLEMENTING THE HOME-SCHOOL APPROACH

In order to adequately understand complex interactions of home-school settings and the interplay of belief, structure, and developmental influences the therapist must gather information about each of the three areas discussed above and evaluate their congruence across components. Also, adequate assessment makes intervention design and modification relatively simple. The therapist should understand that information gathering is a process of structurally mapping the home-school-child processes. The focus is on the interactional sequence within family and school and between family and school around the presenting problem and related issues that led to treatment. The information of interest is the types of complimentary actions between home and school and the sequence of their occurrence (Breunlin & Schwartz, 1986).

Information may also be needed from relevant agencies or professionals outside the home-school systems, such as a neurologist, speech and language therapist, and so forth. This information is needed not only for its contribution to intervention design, but because it gives the therapist access to competing explanations of why the child is failing.

In order to design an appropriate intervention the therapist needs to gather some specifics during contact with the different system members. The specific information needed is outlined below and should be obtained in successive meetings (1-3 per subsystem for assessment—sometimes several other sessions are needed to prepare the family to be able to make the best use of the home-school meeting[s]).

Gathering Family Information

The therapist must carefully observe the centrality of family members and other significant persons, such as friends, grandparents and step-parents. The extent to which they are involved in the problem and solution planning (physically present *or* as influential advisors) needs to be assessed and whether they need to be included in any meetings determined. Second, each family member's view of the problem's cause and previously attempted solutions should be obtained to understand the extent of agreement and where differences occur. An individual interview with the child often helps as it provides the therapist with information on the child's general level of independent functioning, his or her view of the problem, and the individually oriented attempted solutions, if any. Third, the "beliefs" of the family about schools and education should be elicited with special emphasis on where and when intra-familial conflict about these occurs. Fourth, willingness of the family to work with school officials and in what manner needs to be assessed. Often this includes determining where the family, especially parents, view themselves hierarchically in regard to teachers.

Preliminary individual therapy and/or group therapy may also be necessary at this time to engage the student in supportive social or academic skill-building groups. In addition, the child may not be realizing his or her potential because of a learning disability or poor academic skills. Appropriate services should be secured and supported in order to minimize the learning problem's negative impact. Family therapy sessions to help focus on the school problem's meaning to the family and pave the way for resolving belief, structure, and developmental problems may also be needed.

Gathering School Information

Teachers are invaluable members of the evaluation process and are usually the most efficient as well as the most fruitful sources for the school component of the assessment. They can provide critically needed information about the child's academic performance and school behavior. Personal contact with the teacher, and if possible, observation of the child in the school environment will not only provide a richer understanding, but also is an opportunity to engage the teacher in the problem-solving collaboration. Because teachers often assume professional responsibility for a child's school problem, it is important to get their opinions. It is important to do so while treating teachers as professionals providing consultation to you rather than as personally motivated and below you hierarchically in the therapeutic system.

We have found that asking teachers to complete behavioral inventories to be followed up by a face-to-face meeting is a good method for gathering teacher's data in a "professional manner." In addition, behavioral checklists completed by both teacher and parents can be useful in evaluating and comparing the child's behavior in the classroom and at home. The use of similar forms from each source provides a method to bring parents and teachers together in the initial session's discussion under a problem-solving orientation while minimizing blame-placing and defensive orientations (e.g., is it the school's or the parents' fault?). Also, as the number of school personnel involved in the problem increases (e.g., as grade gets

insert 5-5 hee.

higher) the number can overwhelm parents. By having all or several complete the behavioral checklist and consulting with them separately from the meetings with parents, there is less necessity for each teacher to be at or speak at the home-school meeting. However, all teachers with significant influence on the actual implementation and maintenance of the problem should be included in the home-school meeting.

Gathering Home-School Information

At a home-school level the therapist needs to understand the history of previous communications about the problem, especially whether it was initially labeled a problem by school or parents and the level of agreement that the child has a problem. Eliciting information about attempted collaborations, contacts and other attempted solutions is also important. Perhaps most critical is observing interactions as the joint interviews begin to determine the patterns between system members which serve to maintain the problem or prohibit its solution. Implementation of effective intervention rests squarely on the assessment steps outlined above, and use of information gathering to develop rapport ("join") with each key player of the family and school. This information allows reframing of any attributed "malevolent" motivations and securing overt agreement that the mutual goal is helping the child behave and achieve better in school.

Parents and teachers can be engaged to come to the assessment and subsequent meetings by framing their presence as an indication of concern and interest in solving the child's problem. Each is encouraged to negotiate from a position of strength and mutual respect during previous separate sessions. In approaching the family, the therapist is advised to assure the parents that the focus of treatment will be a means for changing the child's behavior rather than blaming the parents for creating or maintaining the problem. Likewise, in approaching the teacher or school personnel, the therapist should be careful to emphasize the good intentions and previous efforts at helping the child. Further, it is usually easier to elicit cooperation from teachers when the meeting and planned interventions focus on behavior management and concrete, school-related goals, *not* on the personality of the teacher or ad-hoc consultation on teaching practices (Szmuck, Docherty, & Ringness, 1979).

Convening the Home-School Meeting

Following from the literature and our experience, after the initial assessment interviews, it is crucial to convene at least one meeting of the family and school system members in order to concretize and implement a collaborative solution to the presenting problem. This meeting is the critical central session for enabling change of structure, belief, and/or developmental problems maintaining the problem.

If the therapist works in the school he/she may be seen as an agent of the school. If this is the case it is important to have met a couple of times with the family, preferably in their home, prior to the home-school meeting which must almost always be at school. This going to the home, itself, may begin to bridge the gap between both systems. Similarly, therapists that work in non-school settings may initially meet with the family in their office, but should go to the school alone to meet with teachers at least once prior to convening the home-school meeting.

Scheduling is also important. A meeting early in the morning is least disruptive to both parents' and teachers' workday.

The following sequential components comprise the central home-school meeting.

1. *Frame the problem as behavior management and develop responsibilities*. Interventions at this meeting should focus on behavior management rather than academic training. The latter should be considered the province of the school and/or tutors. In particular, inconsistencies about behavior management in the home or between school and home should be minimized or eliminated and supervision increased.

2. *Develop a collaborative plan*. A collaborative plan is developed and implemented by using the shared concerns for the child but dividing responsibilities between parents, teachers, and child. The specific *different* roles need to be developed mutually and be supportive of each other. A prototypic example is having the parent

monitor a child's working at homework for a given period of time, while in the school the teacher may be asked to send home a written assignment sheet to help the parent's monitoring (see what the assignments are that need to be completed). The child's responsibility is to bring home the work and work at it for the prescribed time. It is important, however, that the parents *not* be given the task of checking the quality of the child's work. That should be left for teachers. Similarly, teachers are not given permission or responsibility to monitor home activities.

In addition to establishing complimentary assigned roles and responsibilities, it is important for the parents to give permission to the teacher to hold the child responsible for failure to complete work or for misbehavior. Parents need to know that their expectations of achievement and good in-school behavior and at-home monitoring are adequate and necessary contributions for the teacher to enable their child to learn. It is best if this message comes from the primary teacher or higher school official rather than the therapist.

3. *Implement the plan tentatively.* To help reduce pessimism and enhance communication planned contact between home and school 2-3 weeks for the first week is suggested. It is best if a brief follow-up meeting of the therapist, home, and school can occur to monitor implementation. Problems can be assessed at that time and needed adjustments introduced.

4. *Secure maintenance and follow-up.* Follow-up and maintenance of collaborative procedures in and between home and school settings should be a planned part of this central session. The extent or need for these, their form, and frequency will largely depend upon thoroughness of the assessments and framing of the problem and the clarity of roles/tasks for parents, school personnel, and child. The therapist's ongoing work with both settings will solidify treatment effects by enhancing continuation, rapid implementation of needed modifications, and continued joint "ownership" of the solution. Post-meeting work can also include continued family and marital therapy as indicated, coordinating support services, and continuing work with the school. The latter activity is to ensure the

collaborative definitions of the problem are maintained and proactive approaches to similar subsequent crises occurs.

CASE EXAMPLES

The following case examples exemplify how the Structural/Strategic emphasis on the home-school system works and indicate how to implement the principles presented here.

Case 1

The father had deserted the family several months prior to treatment and mother had become overwhelmed with the responsibilities of raising her three children. As she became more depressed, an inordinate amount of the caretaking fell to the oldest child, and he began to neglect his homework. This led to the school contacting the mother and asking her to put pressure on him to do his homework and become more motivated. Over the year this pattern escalated. The more the school pursued the mother, including eventually threatening expulsion of the boy, the less available she became.

In intervening through a collaborative meeting between the home and school, the therapist helped the mother articulate her concerns and constraints. School officials were able to agree to withhold suspension as "last chance." Given a measure of emotional support from the therapist, combined with an agreed upon simple intervention of her making sure her son set aside one hour per night for homework, the mother was able to respond to the needs of the school. As she became more actively involved in his school achievement she became less depressed. This spurred a renewed sense of confidence in herself. In time, she resumed more of her parental role at home and school, allowing the child to attend to his studies, and maintained a collaborative relationship with the school.

Case 2

A second type of common school problem is exemplified by the following case. James's oppositional and overactive behavior caused innumerable problems at home and in school. The parents frequently would get into arguments where the father accused the mother of being too easy and overprotective and the mother accused the father of being too tough on the child. In school, the teacher would repeatedly complain about the child's distractibility, overactive behavior, and underachievement. Antagonism between home and school increased as the teacher's insistence on parental intervention or referral to a special education program increased. To relieve the growing pressure, the family agreed to a psychological evaluation. Results of the evaluation showed strong evidence of an attention deficit disorder with hyperactivity. Several family sessions were held to bring the mother up in the family hierarchy and to strengthen intergenerational boundaries. In convening the school and the family together to give the results formally and develop an intervention plan, the therapist was confronted with several problems. Because of the family's traditional background and the philosophy of the school, both had an expectation of "discipline and respect" from James, to which he could not conform. They believed James was willfully not paying attention. Given these beliefs, the therapist used the meeting to educate both settings as to the neurological ramifications of James's difficulties and tie these ramifications to the reasons for the home-school conflict. In addition, specific behavioral guidelines were shared with the school and the family in these joint sessions, to help James lengthen the time he attended to tasks, and to channel his high level of activity more appropriately. For example, the parents and the teacher were asked to limit excessive visual stimulation in his learning environment. A behavior management approach using positive reinforcement strategies which rewarded appropriate performance across settings in the same manner was also implemented.

Assuming competence on everyone's part, the therapist respectfully challenged previous assumptions that James was unable to follow rules (once structured) and the effectiveness of methods used to manage James's behavior (negative attention). Moreover, bringing the home and school together allowed a cooperative effort focused on developing clear expectations that were consistent across settings and eliminated blame and felt intractable conflict. This complimentary orientation took the place of the adversarial relationship that had previously existed. The boy's behavior and performance improved steadily in the months following.

REFERENCES

Atkeson, B.M. & Forman, R. (1979). Home based reinforcement programs designed to modify classroom behavior: A review and methodology evaluation. *Psychological Bulletin*, *53*, 1298-1308.

Aponte, H.J. (1976). The family school interview. *Family Process*, *15*, 303-310.

Baker, H.S. (1979). The conquering hero quits: Narcissistic factors in underachievement and failure. *American Journal of Psychotherapy*, *33*, 37-42.

Breunlin, D. & Schwartz, R. (1986). Sequences: Toward a common denominator of family therapy. *Family Process*, *25*, 67-87.

Brophy, J.E. & Evertson, C. (1981). *Student characteristics and teaching*. New York: Longman.

Caplan, G. (1970). *The theory and practice of consultation and education*. Palo Alto: National Press Books.

Carter, E. & McGoldrick, M. (Eds.) (1988). *The family life cycle and family therapy* (2nd edition). New York: Gardner Press.

Coleman, J.S. (1966). *Equality of educational opportunity*. U.S. Department of Health Education and Welfare, Number 38001.

Combrinck-Graham, L. (1985). A family model of development. *Family Process*, *24*, 139-150.

Eno, M. (1985). Children with school problems: A family therapy perspective. In R. Ziffer (Ed.) *Adjunctive techniques of family therapy*. Orlando, FL: Grune & Stratton.

Falicov, C. & Karrer, B. (1980). Cultural variations in the family life cycle: The Mexican American Family. In E. Carter & M. McGoldrick (Eds.) *The family life cycle and family therapy*. New York: Gardner Press.

Garbarino, J. (1982). *Child and family in the social environment*. New York: Aldine Press.

Good, T. (1980). Classroom expectations: Teacher pupil interaction. In J.H. McMillan (Ed.) *The social psychology of school learnings*. New York: Academic Press.

Gutkin, T.B. (1981). Related frequency of consultee lack of knowledge, skills, confidence and objectivity in school settings. *Journal of School Psychology*, *19*, 57-61.

Haley, J. (1976). *Problem solving therapy*. San Francisco: Jossey-Bass.

Johnson, D.W. (1980). Group processes: The influence of student-student interactions on school outcomes. In J.H. McMillan (Ed.) *The social psychology of school learning*. New York: Academic Press.

Kessler, J.W. (1966). *Psychopathology of childhood*. Englewood Cliffs, NJ: Prentice-Hall.

Kessler, M. & Albee, G.W. (1975). Primary Prevention. In M.R. Rosenzweig & L.W. Porter (Eds.) *Annual review of psychology*, *vol 26*. Palo Alto: Annual Reviews.

Liddle, H.A. (Ed.) (1983). *Clinical implications of the family cycle*. Rockville, MD: Aspen Systems Corporation.

Lusterman, D.D. (1985). An eco-systemic approach to family school problems. *The American Journal of Family Therapy*, *13*, 22-30.

McCubbin, H. & Dahl, B. (1975). *Marriage and family: Individuals in life cycles*. New York: J. Wiley.

McGuire, D. & Cimmarusti, R. (1986). *A topology for the intercontextual assessment and treatment of school related problems*. Unpublished manuscript available from the first author at the Institute for Juvenile Research, 907 S. Wolcott, Chicago, IL 60612.

McGuire, D. & Lyons, J. (1985). A transactional model for underachievement school problems. *American Journal of Family Therapy*, *13*, 37-45.

McGuire, D. & Tolan, P. (1988). Clinical interventions with large family systems: Balancing interests through siblings. In M. Kahn & K. Lewis (Eds.) *Siblings in therapy*. New York: Norton Press.

Minuchin, P., Biber, B., Shapiro, E., & Zimiles, H. (1969). *The psychological impact of the school experience*. New York: Basic Books.

Minuchin, S. & Fishman, H.C. (1981). *Family Therapy Techniques*. Cambridge, MA: Harvard University Press.

Rutter, M. (1983). School effects on pupil progress: Research findings policy implications, *Child Development*, *54*, 1-29.

Santa-Barbara, J., Woodward, C.A., Levin, S., Goodman, J.T., Steiner, D. & Epstein, N.B. (1979). The McMaster family therapy outcome study: An overview of methods and results. *International Journal of Family Therapy*, *1*, 304-323.

Sattler, J. (1982). *Assessment of children's intelligence and special abilities* (2nd edition). Boston: Allyn & Bacon.

Scheinfeld, D.R. (1983). Family relationships and school achievement among boys of lower income urban black families. *American Journal of Orthopsychiatry*, *53*, 127-143.

Szmuck, M.I.C., Docherty, E., & Ringness, T. (1979). Behavioral objectives for psychological consultations in the school. *Psychology in the Schools*, *16*, 143-148.

Tolan, P.H., Cromwell, R., & Brasswell, M. (1986). The application of family therapy to juvenile delinquency: A critical review of the literature. *Family Process*, *25*, 619-649.

Tolan, R., Ryan, K., & Jaffe, C. (1985). Adolescent mental health service use and provider, process and recipient characteristics. *Journal of Child Clinical Psychology*, *17*, 228-235.

Viale-Val, G., Rosenthal, R.H., Curtiss, G., & Marohn, R.C. (1984). Dropout from adolescent psychotherapy: A preliminary study. *Journal of the American Academy of Child Psychiatry*, *23*, 562-568.

Wood, B. (1985). Proximity and hierarchy: Orthogonal dimensions of family interconnections. *Family Process*, *24*, 347-357.

Children with Chronic Illness:
A Structural-Strategic Family Approach

Christopher J. Brophy
M. Ellen Mitchell

SUMMARY. Structural-Strategic family treatment of the family and child with chronic illness presents a unique challenge to the therapist. This paper reviews the salient issues that influence the conceptualization and treatment of the family with a child with chronic illness. The paper suggests that knowledge of noncompliance with medical regimens, medical aspects of chronic illness, normal childhood development, and Structural-Strategic family concepts are necessary for the family therapist treating these families. Examples of treatment techniques are provided and illustrated with case presentations.

Chronic illness in a child has the potential to be a major disrupting force on family functioning. It can present a variety of problems for the family including, increased insurance premiums and other financial burdens, need for additional employment by one or both parents to accommodate increased financial demands, inconveniences such as taking time off from work for medical appointments, decreased leisure time due to daily demands of the child's medical treatment, and even structural modifications to the house (Johnson, 1985). It is not surprising that childhood chronic illness may result in the disruption of family functioning.

These pressures can impede family functioning in several ways. The child with a chronic illness is at increased risk for behavior problems (Hurtig & White, 1986; Morgan & Jackson, 1986; Wallander, Varni, Babani, Banis, & Wilcox, 1988) and their families may suffer from marital dissatisfaction or discord (Johnson, 1988), parental worry and depression (Drotar, Crawford, & Bush, 1984),

Christopher J. Brophy is in private practice.
M. Ellen Mitchell is affiliated with the Illinois Institute of Technology.

129

and decreased parental involvement with the chronically ill child's siblings (Varni & Wallander, 1988). Despite these findings, the majority of families of chronically ill children adjust well (Turk & Kerns, 1985; Lamanek, Moore, Gresham, Williamson, & Kelly, 1986; Spaulding & Morgan, 1986; Varni & Wallander, 1988).

Whereas, not all families become dysfunctional as a result of the child's chronic illness all families must attend to the child's medical care (Hamburg, 1983; Johnson, 1985; Varni & Babani, 1986). Successful management of chronic illness demands the day-to-day attention of the child and the family. Thus, family functioning must be viewed within the context of the persistent medical demands which accompany the illness. The distinctive characteristics and complexities of these families demand special knowledge and understanding from the family therapist.

The multiple influences which contribute to the complexity of the organization and treatment of these families are summarized in Figure 1. It is the thesis of this paper that periods of relatively adequate adjustment are followed by times of difficulty as a consequence of developmental transitions of the child, the family, and the normal course of the illness (Carter & McGoldrick, 1980; Drotar et al., 1984). These transitions demand new coping methods on the part of the family. The therapist's role is to help the family navigate and anticipate these expectable changes and to differentiate crisis management from more enduring modes of family functioning.

Thus, it is imperative that the family therapist have, as a minimum, working knowledge of the following areas: (1) noncompliance with medical regimens; (2) medical aspects of the chronic illness; (3) normal childhood development; (4) application of Structural-Strategic family methods. A brief introduction to each of these areas will be followed by case illustrations of Structural-Strategic family interventions.

NONCOMPLIANCE WITH MEDICAL REGIMENS

It has been estimated that between 11% and 89% of patients fail to comply with specific treatment recommendations for chronic pediatric conditions (Dunbar, 1983). Failure to comply with the medical regimen may put the child at risk for additional treatment, in-

Figure 1. Factors Affecting Family Functioning and Treatment

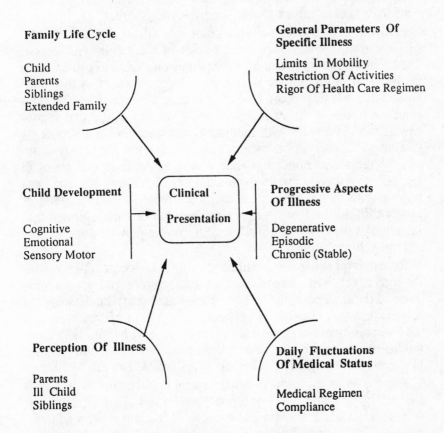

Family Life Cycle

Child
Parents
Siblings
Extended Family

General Parameters Of Specific Illness

Limits In Mobility
Restriction Of Activities
Rigor Of Health Care Regimen

Child Development

Cognitive
Emotional
Sensory Motor

Clinical Presentation

Progressive Aspects Of Illness

Degenerative
Episodic
Chronic (Stable)

Perception Of Illness

Parents
Ill Child
Siblings

Daily Fluctuations Of Medical Status

Medical Regimen
Compliance

cluding medication, further diagnostic testing, additional hospitalizations, and increased health risk (Parrish, 1986; Varni & Babani, 1986). Early noncompliance with medical regimens may lead to serious or even fatal long-term consequences. For example, children with diabetes mellitus are at increased risk for heart attacks, renal failure, and blindness as they age. It is believed that such health risks can be delayed or prevented if control of blood glucose levels is maintained (Johnson, 1988).

Much of the treatment of chronic illness is conducted by the family outside of medical facilities. Long-term inpatient medical care is too disruptive to the family and expensive. A high degree of patient participation in the treatment of these disorders is thus required. This may necessitate extensive family involvement.

Noncompliance affects the health of the child, and the likelihood of psychological and social difficulties in the family (Anderson, 1981; Gath, Smith, & Baum, 1980; Johnson, 1980). Further, poor health in the child may lead to additional stressors such as increased financial strain due to the cost of subsequent treatments. The relationship among these variables is uncertain; it may be that family dysfunction interferes with medical compliance and leads to negative health consequences which in turn may fuel further dysfunction. Alternately, noncompliance may precipitate health crises in the child that lead to family dysfunctioning. In either case, noncompliance with medical regimens may contribute to the likelihood of family difficulties. Thus, promoting compliance with regimens that maintain or improve the child's health may help avoid disturbances in family functioning.

Research on enhancing compliance within the context of the family is relatively rare. Few consistent demographic and person-variables of parental compliance have been found (Parrish, 1986). One relationship that emerges is between the duration of treatment and the complexity of the treatment (Varni & Babani, 1986). Therefore, modifications which simplify treatment demands and convenience may enhance compliance (Dunbar, Marshall, & Hovell, 1979).

Patients and their families cannot easily be dichotomously classified as "good" compliers or "poor" compliers (Parrish, 1986). It seems likely that most families comply with some aspects of treatment and not others (Trostle, Hauser, & Susser, 1983; Webb et al., 1984). Further, a given family's compliance is likely to vary as the illness changes, as members of the family develop, and as the family system evolves.

The patient's perception of their illness and treatment can play a role in determining compliance (Trostle et al., 1983). Other family members, in turn, can influence the perception a patient has of their illness (Turk, Flor, & Rudy, 1987). Family attitudes toward the regimen also may contribute to compliance (Parrish, 1986). Depending on their perceptions and attitudes family members may be more or less likely to become involved in the medical regimen; to remind, assist, or modify the home environment in order to facilitate compliance. Patients and their families are likely, then, to maintain aspects of the regimen they perceive as helpful and discard those aspects that they deem as less so. This may result in a coalition of the family against the health care professionals which can have long-term consequences for the health of the child.

Determinants of noncompliance are also embedded in the more immediate circumstances surrounding the family's daily management of the child's chronic illness. For example, many treatments are aversive. They may be time consuming, taking the child and/or other family members away from more desirable activities. They may be uncomfortable or even painful. In addition, with chronic illnesses, the treatment does not result in cure (Drotar, 1981). Families may become demoralized. Further, the bearing of certain aspects of treatment on the child's well-being are often not clear or immediate. Therefore, there may be little incentive, particularly for the child, to adhere to the treatment. The primary caretaker, typically the mother, must then supply the "motivation" for compliance, despite possibly having low motivation themselves. Therefore, the child's noncompliance can create increased family interaction in the form of cajoling, coaxing, persuasion, sympathy, or coercion. Further, noncompliance may provide other family members with the opportunity to avoid aversive aspects of their lives (e.g., marital difficulties) and focus on less aversive endeavors. For example, a parent may attend to the sick child, avoiding undesirable interactions with his or her spouse, and at the same time, allow siblings to escape supervision and engage in play or T.V. instead of treatment participation.

Many techniques have resulted in better compliance with different medical regimens for a variety of pediatric chronic illnesses (Masek & Jankel, 1982; Parrish, 1986; Varni & Babani, 1986). Techniques such as point-systems, self-monitoring, modeling, and behavioral rehearsal can be incorporated strategically into family treatment (Liebman, Horning, & Berger, 1976). This can result in structural family change through redistribution of family responsibilities (Haley, 1976).

MEDICAL AND TREATMENT ASPECTS
OF CHRONIC ILLNESS

Therapists treating families of the chronically ill child should have knowledge of the medical aspects of the child's specific disorder and its treatment (Drotar, 1981; Johnson, 1985). While many chronic illnesses have several features in common (e.g., lengthy duration and potentially great impact on family) there are significant aspects of each disorder which impact uniquely on the family's functioning (Turk & Kerns, 1985).

A major pertinent dimension along which chronic illnesses vary is the seriousness of the disorder. The seriousness of some illnesses changes over time, some are relatively stable while others vary, and still others are degenerative. Additionally, different illnesses require more frequent hospitalizations, more choices of treatment, have greater likelihood of therapeutic failure, and greater threat of death. The family of a child with hemophilia, for instance, is faced with periodic and frequently unforeseeable hemorrhaging (Varni & Wallander, 1988). Bleeding may raise the possibility of death and may necessitate hospitalization. In addition, the child's joints may at times swell due to the hemorrhaging thereby decreasing physical mobility and increasing dependence on the parents.

Therefore, a first requisite step is to gain knowledge of the demands of the treatment on the family. In doing so, it should be kept in mind that most of these regimens were developed without consideration for their psychosocial impact (Drotar, 1981) and may have a substantial impact on family functioning that is not recognized by the family or those directing the medical care.

Treatment demands on the family vary widely in their complexity, difficulty, frequency, discomfort, and with respect to their impact on other aspects of family functioning (Johnson, 1985). For example, successful control of juvenile diabetes requires insulin injection one or two times daily, urine or blood tests of glucose level up to four times daily, and dietary restrictions (Johnson, 1980, 1988).

The therapist should also be as familiar as possible with other involved health care providers. An interdisciplinary approach, in which participating health care providers have a working knowledge of what each professional can do, is recommended (Varni & Babani, 1986). At a minimum, contact with the child's physician should be initiated so that the therapist can be apprised of the child's medical status. In addition, consultation with the physician can increase compliance through modifications in the treatment regimen without compromising therapeutic effect.

DEVELOPMENTAL CONSIDERATIONS

Children are usually unable to accept complete responsibility for the care of their chronic illness. Younger children may not understand the necessity of treatment, while older children may resent the intrusion on their lives. Cognitive development clearly plays a role in perceptions of health, illness, and treatment (Simeonsson, Buckley, & Monson, 1979). Advancing the understanding of health-related concepts appears to parallel Piaget's stages of cognitive development (Simeonsson et al., 1979). Children under the age of six tend to relate the cause of the illness to events occurring just prior to the onset of illness symptoms. Older children attribute causes to the general concept of infection and later to the idea of microorganisms (Nagy, 1951). Similar developmental differences exist for the understanding of medical treatment (Steward & Regalbutto, 1975).

The complexity of certain aspects of the treatment, too, may be beyond the young child's cognitive or motor abilities. Most nine-year-old diabetics are capable of self-administering their daily insulin injections. Not until the age of 12, however, are most children able to independently monitor their glucose level through urine testing (Johnson, 1982). Educating parents about the practical implications of normal childhood development can assist the parents in determining appropriate treatment responsibilities for their children.

The capabilities of most chronically ill children are in continuous development. They will be constantly gaining more ability to be responsible for the management of medical regimens and care of themselves. As the child develops he/she will probably demand, and in most cases should receive, increasing responsibility for the daily management of their treatment. Thus, because of the long-term nature of chronic illness, the family must undergo frequent changes in carrying out the treatment requirements even if the actual medical requirements go unchanged. Noncompliance often arises at times of developmental shift in management capabilities.

Awareness of developmental considerations can help prevent foreseeable difficulties. Preparing the family for these changes may help to smooth over these transitions and avoid potential difficulties. Further, the recognition of, and emphasis on, expected and unrealized developmental changes in self-care and responsibility can be incorporated in Structural-Strategic interventions.

STRUCTURAL-STRATEGIC CONCEPTS

Structural-Strategic therapy for a family with a child who has a chronic illness proceeds in a manner quite similar to that for any family with a child focused problem (Minuchin, 1974; Haley, 1976; Madanes, 1981; Minuchin & Fishman, 1982). There are, however, basic issues quintessentially bound with the illness which change the emphasis, thus modifying the approach.

Minuchin's (1984) original definition of family structure focused on consolidation of the functional demands which organize the interactions of family members. Structure is the composite of subsystems which in turn are mediated by boundaries or rules which define the participatory roles of individual members. Thus, family interactional style may be characterized in terms of roles and boundaries.

Roles

Adequate flexibility with respect to roles is essential to healthy family functioning (Whitaker, 1976). Families with a chronically ill child are particularly at-risk for the development of rigid roles (Sargent & Liebman, 1985; Minuchin, Baker, Rosman, Liebman, Millman & Todd, 1975). The demands of the medical regimen may promote rigidity of roles. Family roles then become defined around the illness (Bartholomew, 1986) and the needs of the ill child, rather than the needs of the whole family. The mother may be the only family member available to attend and/or transport the child to multiple medical/therapy appointments. This may be because the father is working overtime to increase income to meet financial demands related to the illness. As the father is increasingly bound to the role of wage earner, so is the mother more tied into the caretaker role.

There are several roles which family members tend to lock into when chronic illness is present. The most apparent are the roles of caretaker and sick child. Typically, these are assigned to the mother and the child respectively and exclusively. These roles may be limiting and self-perpetuating. The caretaker may assume duties which are better delegated; the sick child may abdicate responsibility for self-care. Other activities of the child may be overshadowed. The siblings' roles are generally manifest in one of two ways. The first is best described as underinvolvement. In this situation, healthy brothers and sisters are virtually excluded or dismissed from caretaking and other illness related activities. In the extreme they may be emotionally and behaviorally cut off from the child with the chronic illness. Their responsibility is to limit the attention and time they need from the parents. The second role involves over-active caretaking and taking on parental responsibilities. They become involved as secondary caretakers at the expense of other activities such as time with peers. It is important for the therapist to help the family escape simplified exclusive roles, and negotiate a structural organization that can respond to the tensions imposed by the medical needs. One important step is to help the parents determine the appropriate roles for siblings in accordance with age, maturity, and individual needs, and give siblings permission to function in those roles. Similarly, the family must adopt a coping style that can adjust roles to fit variations in needs during times of relative stability as compared to times of health crisis.

All too often family members become stuck in a given role and subsequent manner of interacting; for example, the ill child must be weak, and the well child strong and responsible. Assigning new roles as an "experiment" or the use of role sharing is a good method for structurally disrupting fixed patterns (Haley, 1976). An example might be reassignment of the "job" of caretaking to another family member and/or strategically instructing the sick child to try taking some of the burden of being "no bother" from a sibling so that the brother or sister can "have their turn being cared for." Thus, family members are prompted to take on new roles, relinquish old ones, and be flexible in their family role.

Proximity

Unclear interpersonal boundaries emanate from an imbalance in interpersonal closeness or proximity. Change occurs along the dimensions distance and closeness in the natural course of normal development and with different stages of the illness. Families are at risk for confusion of proximity because periods of exacerbation of the illness demand greater parental involvement with the child. Consequently disengagement from other family members may occur. When this occurs, the marital dyad and the healthy siblings are at risk for exclusion from interaction with the primary caretaker and/or the ill child. It should be borne in mind that during times of health crisis and need, this is a necessary family organization. The possibility of dysfunction in the family increases when these roles become fixed patterns of interaction. As described below, it is also problematic when these patterns breach generational hierarchies.

Marital conflict is a frequent concomitant of family life with a chronically ill child (Drotar et al., 1984; Breslau, Staruch, & Mortimer, 1982). Competing demands may give rise to neglect of other responsibilities and place the marital relationship at risk. Factors related to the severity of the illness, stage of the illness, prognosis, the family's past experience with the illness, and the functional level of the child may lead the caretaker to remain overly invested in and worried about the child (Minuchin et al., 1975; Breslau et al., 1982; Lewis & Khaw, 1982; Sargent & Liebman, 1985) and decrease their involvement with their spouse. While not the focus of this paper, the marital relationship should be assessed and if appropriate, monitored by the therapist.

As mentioned earlier, the natural course of development, as well as specific aspects of the child's illness, place changing demands on the family (Walker, Ford, & Donald, 1987). One common problem is that family operations become organized around the illness and its management at a particular point in the development of the illness or the child, rather than around the sick child and/or the family as a whole. This is a subtle but important distinction; to rally around a family member is important, to organize statically around an illness is problematic. Thus, it is not the presence of the illness which creates family dysfunction but rather the impact of the illness and the demands of the treatment on family functioning.

Hierarchy and Boundaries

Hierarchy commonly refers to generational boundaries. Difficulties in boundary definition and hierarchical alignment may occur related to nurturance and control (Wood & Talmon, 1983). Problems with nurturance arise when a parent becomes overly involved with one child. This may be expected in families when they have to face a life threatening illness (Sargent & Liebman, 1985; Lewis & Khaw, 1982). Unfortunately, overinvolvement may have consequences for the sick child in the form of adultification or infantilization (Foster, 1986). In these situations, the behavioral expectations or demands placed on the child are at a level which is either significantly below or above the child's developmental age. For example, the parent who forbids their child to visit at a friend's house because of unfounded fears regarding the child's health is engaging in infantilization. Placing too high or too low expectations on the child for self-care is another example of problems with nurturance which potentially affect compliance with the medical regimen and in turn disrupt family functioning.

A sometimes useful intervention for infantilization is to ask the child to pretend to be distressed when they do not actually feel bad. The parent must then attempt to determine when the child is in real distress or need. The technique of pretending forces the parent to react to symptoms in a new way and to view the child as more able to understand and control their illness (Madanes, 1981; 1984). This intervention must be used carefully and strategically after extensive joining with the family and judgement about the medical stability of the child. It would not be appropriate in cases where the child might actually have a life threatening situation which could be misinterpreted.

Problems with control arise when too much power is accorded a child in making family decisions. Walker et al. (1987) found that mothers of children with chronic illness were less inclined to be strict when the child was severely ill as compared to times when the child was in better health. Children may also pretend to be ill and attempt to manipulate their parents (Peterson, 1972). Hierarchical reversal, or cross generational alliances, may be both necessary and functional for the family as an essential concomitant to caretaking (Drotar et al., 1984). Sensitive to the needs and wants of the chronically ill child, and coupled with a strong sense of lack of control and dependency, the family may allow the child to direct the family inappropriately. The result is a family prone to boundary disturbance (Ritchie, 1981) in which members take on roles which are inconsistent with their place of power in the family.

Families with a chronically ill child are often required to engage in health care regimens which may be monotonous, difficult, embarrassing to the child, and painful. This may lead families to be reluctant to make time unrelated to health care unpleasant by the imposition of rules, requests, and responsibilities. While the needs and sentiments which undergird the inverted hierarchy are understandable, it is important for the parents to hold the child responsible for misbehavior and to be able to discipline as necessary.

Reframing this tendency is an excellent technique for making palatable that which might otherwise be quite distasteful. For instance, the therapist may reframe limit setting as a method of education. In this manner, the parent can interpret limit setting as teaching their child about living in a world of hierarchies and responsibility as opposed to mere punishment. Another important method of intervention is to involve the child and siblings in the formation of rules and consequences as a strategic way of allowing them to have control while also realigning the power in the hierarchy back towards the parents. Behavioral techniques such as point-systems or contingency contracts may be strategically incorporated into structural treatment (Liebman et al., 1976). Such techniques make explicit the duties, responsibilities, and roles of family members and may be particularly useful when communication among family members has broken down (Haley, 1976).

Coalitions and Alliances

Dysfunctional family coalitions between two or more members against another are common in families with problems in which chronic childhood illness is present (Penn, 1983; Bartholomew, 1986). Rigid roles frequently give rise to dysfunctional coalitions (Drotar et al., 1984). For example, in response to the primary caretaker's extensive involvement with the sick child the caretaker's spouse may form an alliance with the healthy children (Penn, 1983). The two coalitions tend to work against one another rather than cooperatively. This results in what may appear to be two families: one organized around illness related activities and the other around non-illness activity. The ensuing fragmentation precludes whole family functioning.

The development of dysfunctional rather than strategic coalitions with health care professionals may also disrupt family functioning (Berger & Jurkovic, 1984; Coopersmith, 1982; Penn, 1983). Problems with medical compliance and wishes to inveigle cooperation must be monitored so that the therapist is not inadvertently co-opted. These alliances are quite functional when they are formed but through time they may fail to develop according to changing needs. Obtaining permission from the parents for periodic communication with the pediatrician will help to keep the therapist apprised of the extent to which the family is involved with other health care professionals.

There are a number of "generic" structural interventions which can be useful for rectifying dysfunctional coalitions (Aponte & VanDeusen, 1981). For example, it is often important, in session, to change actual seating of family members in order to disrupt coalitions and realign subsystems. The therapist may also act to support a given family member through the technique of unbalancing. For example, the therapist can provide selective attention to a given family member to create a new alliance and disrupt an old one.

While these interventions are not unique to these families, the issues which give rise to the problems are. The therapist is at-risk for misidentifying family roles and structures as dysfunctional. Structures, which in other families would be identified as problematic, may serve an important function in families with children with chronic illness. The illness may demand that family members be intimately involved with one another in ways that depart from conventional family interactions and roles, as in the case when an older child needs help bathing. The therapist's knowledge about the illness, its treatment, and issues of compliance can enhance evaluation of the family structure. It is important to determine if the observed structure is temporary in response to an acute crisis or rigidified in such a way as to be an impediment to daily demands and developmental transition of all members. The presence of structural anomalies is not in and of itself suggestive of dysfunction (Drotar et al., 1984).

Subsystems

The notion of subsystems is central to Structural-Strategic family therapy and essential for understanding treatment for families with a chronically ill child (Drotar et al., 1984). One difference between families with a chronically ill child and families with other child centered problems is the involvement of non-family systems as well as extended family (Foster, 1986). Health care professionals represent a subsystem which moves in and out of the family depending on the medical needs of the child at any given time. The physician is traditionally accorded the role of power and authority and is placed uppermost in the hierarchy (Greiner, 1984). The physician, in turn, endows nurses, therapists, and other health professionals with this power. There is a delicate balance, however, between parental authority, child autonomy, and family functioning. The family cannot simply allow the health care professionals to assume family responsibilities, nor would most medical providers wish such control. The family must turn to professionals for guidance, advice, direction and education without becoming overly dependent upon these relationships.

Similarly, medical crisis can bring grandparents and other extended family members into the family for long periods of time. This may inadvertently disrupt the normal establishment of relationships and create new subsystems or coalitions (Carter & McGoldrick, 1980).

Life Cycle

Families are most at risk during times of transition (Haley, 1976; Minuchin, 1974). This applies to families with a child with chronic illness as well. The presence of a child with a chronic illness does not preclude satisfactory family functioning and must be viewed within the frame of normal family development (Walker et al., 1987; Venters, 1981).

Thus, as has been noted in the literature (Walker et al., 1987; Drotar et al., 1984) preschool years and adolescence, when independence is a salient developmental issue, can be particularly difficult when nurturance, control, limited autonomy, and weakened personal boundaries are pulled for by the medical problem. The therapist's understanding of normal child and family development will allow him/her to guide the family through these transitions as well as prepare the family for potentially problematic transitions in the future.

Structural concepts and techniques are thus utilized in session with the child and family to create a family structure that is more functional by being flexible enough for crises as well as stable periods and which can help the family anticipate expectable transitions. Strategic methods, both in session and in out-of-session homework assignments, foster medical compliance and more effective family operations overall. Through their use, the therapist can optimize the autonomy of the ill child, realign generational boundaries and hierarchy, and free up family members from rigid roles.

CASE ILLUSTRATIONS

Case I

Terry, age 13, had juvenile onset diabetes. She was one of two children; her older sister had recently left home to attend college. Her parents brought her for outpatient psychotherapy following an episode of emergency medical treatment for diabetic ketoacidosis because she had failed to adhere to her prescribed diet.

The mother initiated the session with a long litany of Terry's dietary failures, her tendency to stay out late with friends, and her lack of responsibility to the family. While the mother spoke, Terry and her father sat silently; occasionally making furtive eye contact. The father stated the problem was that Terry wasn't getting along with her mother. Terry retorted that her mother was "bugging" and "babying" her by not allowing her to get her own lunch at school with friends. Instead, the mother would prepare special lunches and insist they must be eaten. Terry believed this resulted in negative appraisal by peers. It was readily apparent that normal developmental change, in the form of the recent move of the older sister, in combination with Terry's move into adolescence, was creating tension in the family. The mother was having difficulty adjusting to the loss of her role as mother and caretaker to her daughters. The father had withdrawn from the family and was having difficulty reentering into relationships with his daughters and wife. These transitions towards greater independence were confused and impeded by concerns about Terry's illness.

It was ascertained that Terry understood the rationale and requirements of her dietary regimen. Treatment thus began with an attempt to reframe Terry's "rebellion" as normal attempts to be responsible and independent. Terry's seating in session was shifted from a position between her parents. Agreements were made for Terry to cook some of the family meals to demonstrate her competence to her parents and to allow her mother to observe her eating habits in a somewhat less intrusive manner. Verbalizations by the father were selectively attended to encourage his involvement with his wife as a partner. The parents were enjoined to reach an agreement regarding a food budget for Terry to allow her to buy lunches provided that she accounted for the money. In this manner, attention was shifted from the content of what she ate to financial and dietary responsibility. Terry also expressed her sadness and feelings of loss related to her sister leaving home. The family entered into a discussion of parameters for Terry to be able to "earn" an overnight visit with her sister. Subsequent to these sessions, Terry admitted to one episode of inappropriate diet and money use. Medical intervention was not required and the problem apparently remained resolved.

Case II

Davie was a six-year-old boy who had a congenitally defective bladder that required extensive reconstructive surgery. His condition demanded daily catheterization to flush the bladder, albeit he could urinate in the usual manner. Failure to follow the regimen resulted in involuntary urination and risk for infection. He presented with his mother, father, brother age 11, and sister age 9 at the instigation of his father. The presenting complaint revolved around the fact that he was wetting himself almost daily.

An initial interview revealed a father very concerned about his son with a tendency to be overly controlling and perfectionistic as evidenced by repeated admonishments to be well behaved. He spoke in a similarly officious manner to his wife who would respond with silence. Both the brother and sister had decreased their play time with Davie because tickling, wrestling, or vigorous romping would result in urination. The brother was reluctant to be seen with Davie and the sister had taken on many caretaking functions, hoping to help her brother hide the problem. The father worked ten-hour days and expressed anger that his wife didn't take care of the problem. The mother was also employed and felt that given the nature of the problem her husband should be more involved.

Davie was remarkably articulate for his age regarding the details of his health care regimen but expressed the need and desire for assistance. The parents were instructed to discuss options for helping their son. After they were able to generate several useful ideas, the therapist strategically suggested that this might be a task appropriately delegated to the older son. They agreed that the older brother would help for the next week on a regular basis and then be available for consultation or actual physical assistance to his brother if Davie asked in the following weeks. This served to strengthen the male sibling subsystem as well as the parental decision making role. It also blocked the sister from increasing her caretaker role. She in turn was encouraged to take on the role of playmate which was more fitting her age. Wetting decreased to twice in the first week and zero times the second. Other family issues surfaced at this time and the family was seen further to help with these problems. Wetting did not recur.

SUMMARY

These cases illustrate the complexities of treatment for families with a child with chronic illness. Structural-Strategic approaches provide a good model for the conceptualization and treatment of these families. These approaches, in combination with knowledge of the parameters of medical compliance, the medical regimen, the specific illness, and family and child development, allow the family therapist to assess and intervene effectively. It should be reiterated that it is not the chronic illness nor presence of unusual family structures which signal family dysfunction. Instead, it is the impact of the illness on the family and the persistence of structures no longer indicated that create problems for these families.

REFERENCES

Anderson, B., Miller, J., Auslander, W., & Santiago, J. (1981). Family characteristics of diabetic adolescents: Relationship to metabolic control. *Diabetes Care, 4*, 586-594.

Aponte, H. J., & VanDeusen, J. M. (1981). Structural family therapy. In A. S. Gurman & D. P. Kniskern (Eds.), *Handbook of family therapy* (pp. 310-360). New York: Brunner/Mazel.

Bartholomew, K. L. (1986). Family therapy for children with chronic illness. In L. Combrinck-Graham (Ed.), *Treating young children in family therapy* (pp. 43-51). Rockville, MD: Aspen Publications.

Berger, M., Jurkovic G. J., & Assoc. (1984). *Practicing psychotherapy in diverse settings*. San Francisco: Jossey-Bass.

Breslau, N., Staruch, K. S., & Mortimer, E. A. (1982). Psychological distress in mothers of disabled children. *American Journal of Diseases of Children, 136*, 682-686.

Carter, E. A., & McGoldrick, M. (1980). The family life cycle and family therapy: An overview. In E. A. Carter & M. McGoldrick (Eds.), *The family life cycle: A framework for family therapy* (pp. 8-20). New York: Gardner Press.

Coopersmith, E. I. (1982). The place of family therapy in the hierarchy of larger systems. In L. Aronson & B. Wolberg (Eds.), *Group and family therapy: 1982, an overview*. New York: Brunner/Mazel.

Drotar, D. (1981). Psychological perspectives of chronic childhood illness. *Journal of Pediatric Psychology, 6*(3), 211-228.

Drotar, D., Crawford, P., & Bush, M. (1984). The family context of childhood chronic illness: Implications for psychosocial intervention. In M. G. Eisenbeg, L. C. Sutkin, & M. A. Jansen (Eds.), *Chronic illness and disability through the lifespan: Effects on self and family* (pp. 103-129). New York: Springer.

Dunbar, J. M. (1983). Compliance in pediatric populations: A review. In P. J. McGrath & P. Firestone (Eds.), *Pediatric and adolescent behavioral medicine* (pp. 210-230). New York: Springer.

Dunbar, J. M., Marshall, G. D., & Hovell, M. F. (1979). Behavioral strategies for improving compliance. In R. B. Haynes, D. W. Taylor, & D. L. Sackett (Eds.), *Compliance in health care* (pp. 174-190). Baltimore: Johns Hopkins University Press.

Foster, M. A. (1986). Families with young disabled children in family therapy. In L. Combrinck-Graham (Ed.), *Treating young children in family therapy* (pp. 62-72). Rockville, MD: Aspen Publications.

Gath, A., Smith, M., & Baum, J. (1980). Emotional, behavioral and educational disorders in diabetic children. *Archives of Disease in Childhood, 55*, 371-375.

Greiner, D. (1984). Hospitals and outpatient clinics. In M. Berger, G. J.

Jurkovic, & Assoc. *Practicing psychotherapy in diverse settings* (pp. 247-270). San Francisco: Jossey-Bass.

Haley, J. (1976). *Problem solving therapy: New strategies for effective family therapy*. San Francisco: Jossey-Bass.

Hamburg, B. A. (1983). Chronic illness. In M. D. Levine, W. B. Carey, A. C. Crocker, & R. T. Gross (Eds.), *Developmental-behavioral pediatrics* (pp. 455-463). Philadelphia: W. B. Saunders.

Hurtig, A. L., & White, L. S. (1986). Psychosocial adjustment in children and adolescents with sickle cell disease. *Journal of Pediatric Psychology, 11*, 411-428.

Johnson, S. B. (1980). Psychosocial factors in juvenile diabetes: A review. *Journal of Behavioral Medicine, 3*, 95-116.

Johnson, S. B. (1988). The family and the child with chronic illness. In D. C. Turk & R. D. Kerns (Eds.), *Health, illness, and families: A life-span perspective* (pp. 220-254). New York: Wiley.

Johnson, S. B. (1985). Diabetes mellitus in childhood. In D. K. Routh (Ed.), *Handbook of pediatric psychology* (pp. 9-31). New York: Guilford.

Lemanek, K. L., Moore, S. L., Gresham, F. M., Williamson, D. A., & Kelley, M. L. (1986). Psychological adjustment of children with sickle cell anemia. *Journal of Pediatric Psychology, 11*, 397-410.

Lewis, B. L., & Khaw, K. (1982). Family functioning as a mediating variable affecting psychosocial adjustment of children with cystic fibrosis. *Journal of Pediatrics, 101*, 636-640.

Lewis, C., Knopf, D., Chastain-Larber, K., Ablin, A., Zoger, S., Matthany, K., Glasser, M., & Pantell, R. (1988). Patient, parent, and physician perspectives on pediatric oncology rounds. Journal of Pediatrics, *112*, 378-384.

Liebman, R., Horning, P., & Berger, H. (1976). An integrated treatment program for psychogenic pain. *Family Process, 15*, 397-405.

Madanes, C. (1981). *Strategic family therapy*. San Francisco: Jossey-Bass.

Madanes, C. (1984). *Behind the one-way mirror: Advances in the practice of strategic therapy*. San Francisco Jossey-Bass.

Masek, B. J., & Jankel, W. R. (1984). Therapeutic adherence. In D. C. Russo & J. W. Varni (Eds.), *Behavioral pediatrics: Research and practice* (pp. 375-395). New York: Plenum.

Minuchin, S. (1974). *Families and family therapy*. Cambridge, MA: Harvard University Press.

Minuchin, S., Baker, L., Rosman, B. L., Liebman, R., Milman, L., & Todd, T. C. (1975). A conceptual model of psychosomatic illness in children. *Archives of General Psychiatry, 32*, 1031-1038.

Minuchin, S., & Fishman, H. C. (1981). *Family therapy techniques*. Cambridge, MA: Harvard University Press.

Morgan, S. A., & Jackson, J. (1986). Psychological and social concomitants of sickle cell anemia in adolescents. *Journal of Pediatric Psychology, 11*, 429-440.

Nagy, M. (1951). Children's ideas of the origin of illness. *Health Education Journal*, *9*, 6-12.

Parrish, J. M. (1986). Parent compliance with medical and behavioral recommendations. In N. Krasnegor, J. Arasteh, & M. Cataldo (Eds.), *Child and health behavior: A behavioral pediatrics perspective* (pp. 453-501). New York: Wiley.

Penn, P. (1983). Coalitions and binding interactions in families with chronic illness. *Family Systems*, *1*, 16-25.

Peterson, E. (1972). The impact of adolescent illness on parental relationships. *Journal of Health and Social Behavior*, *13*, 429-437.

Ritchie, K. (1981). Research note: Interaction in the families of epileptic children. *Journal of Child Psychology and Psychiatry*, *22*, 65-71.

Sargent, J., & Liebman, R. (1985). Childhood chronic illness: Issues for psychotherapists. *Community Mental Health Journal*, *21*, 294-311.

Simeonsson, R., Buckley, L., & Monson, L. (1979). Conceptions of illness causality in hospitalized children. *Journal of Pediatric Psychology*, *4*, 77-84.

Simonds, J. (1976). Psychiatric status of diabetic youth in good and poor control. *International Journal of Psychiatry in Medicine: Psychosocial aspects of patient care*, *7*, 133-151.

Spaulding, B. R., & Morgan, S. B. (1986). Spina Bifida children and their parents: A population prone to family dysfunction? *Journal of Pediatric Psychology*, *11*, 359-374.

Steward, M., & Regalbutto, G. (1975). Do doctors know what children know? *American Journal of Orthopsychiatry*, *45*, 146-149.

Trostle, J. A., Hauser, W. A., & Susser, I. S. (1983). The logic of noncompliance: Management of epilepsy from the patient's point of view. *Culture, Medicine, and Psychiatry*, *7*, 35-56.

Turk, D. C., Flor, H., & Rudy, T. E. (1987). Pain and families. I. Etiology, maintenance, and psychosocial impact. *Pain*, *30*, 3-27.

Turk, D. C., & Kerns, R. D. (1985). The family in health and illness. In D. C. Turk & R. D. Kerns (Eds.), *Health, illness, and families: A life-span perspective* (pp. 1-22). New York: Wiley.

Varni, J. W., & Babani, L. (1986). Long-term adherence to health care regimens in pediatric chronic disorders. In N. Krasnegor, J. Arasteh, & M. Cataldo (Eds.), *Child and health behavior: A behavioral pediatrics perspective* (pp. 502-520). New York: Wiley.

Varni, J. W., & Wallander, J. L. (1988). Pediatric chronic disabilities: Hemophilia and spina bifida as examples. In D. K. Routh (Ed), *Handbook of pediatric psychology* (pp. 190-221). New York: Guilford.

Venters, M. (1981). Familial coping with chronic and severe childhood illness: The case of cystic fibrosis. *Social Science and Medicine*, *15A*, 289-297.

Walker, L. S., Ford, M. B., & Donald, W. D. (1987). Cystic fibrosis and family stress: Effects of age and severity of illness. *Pediatrics*, *79*, 239-246.

Wallander, J. L., Varni, J. W., Babani, L., Banis, H. T., & Wilcox, K. T.

(1988). Children with chronic physical disorders: Maternal reports of their psychological adjustment. *Journal of Pediatric Psychology*, *13*, 197-212.

Webb, K. L., Dobson, A. J., O'Connell, D. L., Tupling, H. E., Harris, G. W., Moxon, J. A., Sulway, M. J., & Leeder, S. R. (1984). Dietary compliance among insulin-dependent diabetics. *Journal of Chronic Diseases*, *37*(8), 633-643.

Whitaker, C. (1976). A family is a four dimensional relationship. In J. P. Guerin (Ed.), *Family therapy* (pp. 182-192). New York: Gardner Press.

Wood, B., & Talmon, M. (1983). Family boundaries in transition: A search for alternatives. *Family Process*, *22*, 347-357.

Guidelines and Pitfalls:
Applying Structural-Strategic Approaches in a Multiple Level Perspective

Patrick H. Tolan

SUMMARY. Key issues in applying a Structural-Strategic view to multi-level interventions with child and adolescent behavior problems are identified and discussed. Guidelines and potential pitfalls in the general approach and the specific methods described in this volume are presented.

The preceding writings provide examples of the general conceptualization of child and adolescent behavior problems from a Structural-Strategic view, with an emphasis on utilizing different system foci in interventions. The specific focus or foci in each piece, is/are determined by the sometimes competing considerations of identifying the most judicious intervention while encompassing enough intervention foci to promote general and lasting change. The material presented has been intended as working guides for application in daily practice, rather than as merely providing a stimulation for thought or comment on therapy. They provide specific applications of the general principles outlined initially (Combrinck-Graham, in press; Tolan, in press) and more fully presented elsewhere (Breunlin & Schwartz, 1986; Haley, 1980; Hoffman, 1981; Minuchin & Fishman; Umbarger, 1983). The most gain from their use depends on adequate familiarity with Structural-Strategic principles and distinction of the specific forms or techniques of intervention from these general principles.

Patrick H. Tolan, PhD, is Associate Professor, Department of Psychology, DePaul University, Chicago, IL 60614.

Therefore, rather than summarize their presentations or re-state previously identified themes, this paper provides, briefly, some additional general guidelines that can aid in applying the techniques and principles provided here and identifies some potential pitfalls that should be avoided.

ADDITIONAL GENERAL GUIDELINES

In addition to the general principles and specific techniques previously presented in this volume, the following are important considerations in applying Structural-Strategic techniques in family therapy with child and adolescent behavior problems.

1. The basic assumption of systemic cause and solution of the problem cannot be abandoned whether working with individuals, consultants outside the family, or subsystems of the family. Otherwise, unproductive blaming and pathologizing of one person or component of the systemic framework will follow.

2. The basic concepts of Structural and Strategic therapy are still excellent guides for therapy, despite recent criticisms and justified emphasis that these are clinical conceptualizations applied by us to guide our work, rather than objective actual qualities of a given family (Breunlin & Schwartz, 1986). It is important to realize the map is not the territory (Hoffman, 1981), but to differentiate that realization from judging the quality and reliability of the map or techniques used to construct it.

3. Tracking sequences of behavior at different systemic levels, to identify how the problem as interaction occurs and is regulated, is still an effective primary concern for any therapeutic endeavor with families with a child behavior problem. However, additional information and reactions to therapist activities provide efficient information about how to modify the sequence emphasized or the meaning the therapist attaches to it. This approach allows emphasis on solutions by changing behaviors without negating contextual, historical, developmental, or extra-familial influences.

4. There are many ways to frame and punctuate a family interaction (or other systemic relations). Similarly, change can be instigated and realized in several ways. For example, intensifying the sequence that promotes a problem is only one method of changing

the sequence. Techniques should be applied by how they fit the situation or the particular family, as well as how congruent they are with the solution "frame" developed. Many families may respond better to less forceful therapeutic approaches, while others may best respond to greater intensity. What should remain constant is the therapist's theoretical conceptualization of the problem.

5. Therapy with behavior problems focuses on partial shifts in behavioral sequences, and will often result in the experience of solutions as "partial" by the family and/or therapist. The change in processes more than complete exorcising of a symptom or problematic sequence is often the realized outcome. Circumscription of when the problem occurs, lesser frequency, slower acceleration to extreme behavior, and quicker recovery or repair are often the steps realized in therapy, with further modification occurring post-therapy. The therapist punctuates these gains and the engendered continued growth as "real change."

ADDITIONAL SPECIFIC PITFALLS

In addition to these guidelines in therapy with behavior problems of children and adolescents, there are also several potential pitfalls, beyond those mentioned in the writings presented here, that merit mentioning and should be avoided.

1. *Being Too Simple Conceptually*. Simply applying general concepts of Structural-Strategic therapy, without considering the specific problem or circumstance of the family is conceptually too simple to be effective most of the time. As argued here, consideration of different presenting problems, levels of organization and influence, and emphasis on careful complex development of the problem's function(s) is important. Assuming that all problem solutions reside fully within families or with modifying specific characteristics of families limits the effectiveness of the therapist and their utility to the family. Conceptual complexity is necessary to be effective with child and adolescent behavior problems (e.g, full elaboration of how the working frame relates to the problem and its solution, careful coordination of the intervention components and its likely effects on constituents, and likely further steps after initial

intervention). Adequate conceptual complexity permits needed clarity and simplicity in intervention implementation.

2. *Being Too Complex in the Intervention.* If the intervention implemented is too complex it is usually because there has been inadequate conceptualizing of the problem and its solution(s). Complexity in the in-session intervention discussions and actions, unclear relationships between the therapist actions and the problem solution, and lack of clarity of why and how directives are to be carried out are all signs of this problem. If these are not occurring, and the intervention implementation still seems too complex, it is probably a reflection of inadequate joining with the family or other pertinent persons. This can lead to unnecessarily cumbersome interactions at least, and dropout or greater problems for the family at worst. To work with a therapist, the family has to understand what they are being asked to do and how it will relieve or solve their problem(s). Also, if the therapist has too complex an intervention to remember, put into action, and/or monitor, he/she is less able to attend to the critical issue of the family's perturbations and subsequent sequences following its articulation and introduction to the family.

3. *Not Considering Extra-Familial Impacts.* As has been emphasized here, it is not always best to focus Structural-Strategic interventions on family interactions or on these interactions alone. Failure to consider the family-extra-familial interface, family subsystems, developmental, social, or other pertinent contextual and circumstance influences can result in muted and unsustained impact. The focus of choice depends on the type of problem, but also on the specific circumstances presented with a given family.

4. *Looking for the Intervention as a Magical Moment.* Videotape editing, charismatic presentations, lucky personal experiences, and/or hearing about lucky experiences from colleagues can produce or perpetuate a myth that Structural-Strategic interventions must impact as a magical moment. "Magic moment" therapeutic effect depends on the wizardry of the therapist, which transforms the system immediately, and eradicates all semblance of problems. Such occurrences are relatively rare in general, but are particularly uncommon when working with child and adolescent behavior prob-

lems. Certainly, such occurrences are not a good method of evaluating therapy's effectiveness. A less hyperbolic version of this view is the idea that interventions are doses of medicine given at a certain rate or precise time to, in and of itself, relieve the family of its "symptom." With behavior problems, careful and often time consuming development of the agreement about the problem to solve, with multiple component intervention, and repeated monitoring and adjusting of application of the interventions are the normal process. Hurrying or grasping at "tricks" is most likely to lead to the family dismissing the therapist, either by dropping out or directly asking for a new therapist.

5. *Dismissing Family and Other's Reports.* Failure to consider the importance of family information can lead to unnecessarily conflicted relationships with the family, what has been termed therapeutic bullying by some. Similarly, information from other professionals, if not given due consideration, is more likely to lead to loss of credibility of the therapist than to the family getting stuck by over-reliance on that information (e.g., child labeled as learning disabled). Respect for the family and others involved and careful reading of feedback from statements, questions, and suggestions are requisites of realizing an adequate frame and intervention.

These guidelines and pitfalls are not intended to be all encompassing but merely highlight considerations the conscientious therapist should consider. Their application is no substitution for the therapist's scrutiny. However, combined with adequate understanding of the basic tenets of the Structural-Strategic approach and the specific concepts and techniques presented in this volume, they can help the interested therapist to be more effective with these too common problems.

REFERENCES

Breunlin, D.C. & Schwartz, R.C. (1986). Sequences: Toward a common denominator of family therapy. *Family Process, 25,* 67-87.

Combrinck-Graham, L. (in press). Accountability in family therapy involving children. *Journal of Psychotherapy and the Family.*

Haley, J. (1980). *Leaving home: The therapy of disturbed young people.* New York: McGraw-Hill.

Hoffman, L. (1981). *Foundations of family therapy: A conceptual framework for systems change*. New York: Basic Books.

Minuchin, S. & Fishman, H.C. (1981). *Family therapy techniques*. Cambridge, MA: Harvard University Press.

Tolan, P. H. (in press). Introduction: Treating behavior problems from a multi-level structural-strategic approach. *Journal of Psychotherapy and the Family*.

Umbarger, C. C. (1983). *Structural family therapy*. New York: Grune & Stratton.

Author Index

Albee, G. 108
Alexander, H. 73
Alexander, J. 35,36,37
Alexander, P. 74,76,77,80
Alter-Reid, K. 71,72
Anderson, B. 132
Anderson, L. 79,80,82
Aponte, H. 111,141
Atkeson, B. 109

Baither, R. 49
Baker, H. 109
Baker, L. 90,136
Banis, H. 129
Babani, L. 129,130,131,132,133,135
Barbera, L. 1
Barret, M. 80,81,83,90
Bartholomew, K. 136,140
Baum, J. 132
Beilke, R. 73
Belfer, M. 10
Berger, H. 133
Berger, M. 141
Berliner, L. 85
Besharov, D. 73
Biaggio, M. 72,76,78,84,85
Biber, B. 109
Black, M. 1
Boatman, B. 72,79,80,84
Boatman, E. 72
Boscolo, L. 53
Boskind-White, M. 89
Boszormenyi-Nagy, I. 10
Brasswell, M. 1,29,116
Breslau, N. 138
Breunlin, D. 2,3,44,119,151,152
Brophy, C. 4,7
Brophy, J. 109

Browne, A. 72
Bulkley, J. 79
Buckley, L. 135
Burgess, A. 72
Bush, M. 129
Byrnes, W. 80

Caplan, G. 109
Carr, A. 52
Carter, B. 77
Carter, E. 114,118,130,142
Cecchin, G. 53
Cimmarrusti, R. 110,116
Cleveland, M. 50
Coleman, J. 108
Combrink-Graham, L. 5,6,9,41,114,118, 151
Conte, J. 77
Coopersmith, E. 141
Crawford, P. 129
Cromwell, R. 1,29,116
Curtiss, G. 33,107

Dahl, B. 114
Docherty, E. 122
Donald, W. 138
Drotar, D. 129,130,133,134,138,139,140, 141,142
Dunbar, J. 130,132

Ellis, D. 51
Eno, M. 108
Epstein, N. 110
Everston, C. 109

Falikov, C. 115

Fairburn, C. 90
Fallon, P. 90
Finkelhor, D. 72,77,78,80
Fishman, H. 2,4,30,36,50,51,112,136,151
Flomenhaft, K. 77
Flor, H. 132
Foote, F. 51
Ford, S. 138
Forman, R. 109
Foster, M. 139,142
Frankel, B. 51
Friedman, A. 50,52
Friedman, R. 51
Friedrich, W. 73,90

Garbarino, J. 109
Gath, A. 132
Gawinski, B. 51
Giaretto, A. 76,80
Giaretto, H. 79,80,82,84,85
Gibbs, M. 71
Giller, H. 40
Gold, E. 72
Gold, M. 31
Good, T. 109
Goodman, J. 110
Grace, P. 5,7
Greiner, D. 142
Gresham, F. 130
Grunebaum, H. 10
Guerney, G. 36
Gutkin, T. 109

Haefle, W. 37
Haley, J. 2,4,36,50,52,62,112,133,136,
   137,140,142,151
Hamburg, B. 130
Handy, L. 72,73,76
Hanson, C. 37
Hartman, C. 72
Hauser, W. 132
Hendin, H. 52
Henggeler, S. 37
Herman, J. 76,77
Herivs, O. 51
Hetherington, E. 35,36

Hoffman, L. 151,152
Hoier, T. 73
Horning, P. 133
Hovell, M. 132
Howe, B. 50,51
Huberty, D. 50
Hurtig, A. 129

Jackson, J. 129
Jacob, T. 36
Jaffe, C. 1,33,107
James, B. 81,82
Jankel, W. 133
Joanning, H. 51
Johnson, D. 109
Johnson, S. 129,130,131,132,134,135
Johnson, T. 36
Jurkovic, G. 34,141

Karrer, B. 115
Kandel, D. 50
Kaufman, E. 50
Kelly, M. 130
Kerns, R. 130,134
Kessler, J. 108
Kessler, M. 108
Khaw, K. 138,139
Krasner, B. 10
Kurtines, W. 51

L'Abate, L. 57
LaForte, J. 53
Lachenmeyer, J. 71
Lamiell, J. 34
Larson, N. 74,77,80
Lemanck, K. 130
Lessing, E. 1
Levin, S. 110
Levine, B. 50
Lewis, B. 138,139
Liddle, H. 114
Liebman, R. 133,136,138,139,140
Loeber, R. 30,31,32,35,40
Lorion, R. 31,32,40,41
Lusterman, D.D. 111

Lyons, J. 108,110,111,117

MacFarlane, K. 72,79
Machotka, P. 77
Madanes, C. 49,50,136,139
Maddock, J. 74,77,80
Manghi, E. 5
Marohn, R. 33
Marohn, R. 107
Marshall, G. 132
Masek, B. 135
Massimo, J. 42
Massoth, N. 71
Mayer, A. 79
Mazza, J. 9
McCubbin, H. 114
McGoldrick, M. 114,118,130,142
McGuire, D. 57,108,110,111,116,117
McIntyre, K. 77
Meyer, L. 75
Milman, L. 136
Minuchin, P. 109
Minuchin, S. 2,4,30,36,90,112,136,138,
    142,151
Mitchell, M. 5,7
Monson, L. 135
Montalvo, B. 36
Moore, S. 130
Morgan, S. 129,130
Morris, M. 51
Morrissey, M. 50
Mortimer, E. 138
Mrazek, P. 72,78
Mulvey, E. 30,40

Nagy, M. 135
Nasjleti, M. 81,82

Olson, D. 82
Orzek, A. 72,73

Palazzoli, M. 53,57
Papper, P. 77
Parrish, J. 131,132,133

Patterson, G. 36,40
Perez-Vidal, A. 51
Pelletier, G. 72,73,76
Penn, P. 140,141
Pentz, M. 40
Peters, J. 72
Peterson, E. 139
Petronio, R. 31
Phelps, P. 30,42
Piercy, F. 51
Pittman, F. 77
Pollinger, A. 52
Pollinger-Hoss, A. 52
Prata, G. 53
Press, S. 37

Quinn, W. 51

Rappaport, J. 34
Regalbutto, G. 135
Reilly, D. 49,50
Reiss, D. 30,35,37
Ribordy, S. 7
Ridberg, E. 35
Ringness, T. 122
Ritchie, K. 140
Roberge, L. 72
Rodicke, J. 37
Root, M. 90
Rorbaugh, M. 37
Rosenthal, R. 33,107
Rosman, B. 36,50,90,136
Rudy, T. 132
Russell, C. 82
Russell, D. 73
Rutter, M. 40,108
Ryan, K. 1,33,107

Saba, G. 90
Santa-Barbara, J. 110
Sargent, J. 136,138,139
Schechter, M. 72
Scheinfeld, D. 108
Schetky, D. 72
Schumer, F. 36

Schwartz, R. 2,3,5,7,90,91,102,119,151, 152
Selekman, M. 5,7,51,56
Seidman, E. 34
Sgroi, S. 74,80
Shafer, G. 79,80,82
Shapiro, M. 109
Shore, M. 42
Siebert, F. 1
Sigal, J. 71
Silverstein, M. 77
Simeonsson, R. 135
Simon, R. 53
Singer, M. 35,36
Smith, M. 132
Solin, C. 79
Spark, G. 10
Spaulding, B. 130
Sprenkle, D. 82
Stanton, M. 49,50,51,52,54,59,61
Staruch, K. 138
Steele, B. 73
Stern, M. 75
Stevens, D. 85
Steward, M. 135
Stouthamer-Loeber, M. 35
Stowie, R. 35
Streiner, M. 110
Susser, I. 132
Swan, R. 80
Swanson, L. 72,76,78,84,85
Sykes, C. 80
Szapoczhik, J. 51,52
Szmuck, M. 122

Talmon, M. 139
Tennen, H. 37
Todd, T. 5,7,50,51,52,53,54,55,136

Tolan, P. 1,5,7,29,31,32,33,34,35,37,40, 42,43,107,116,151
Traicoff, M. 72,74,79,80,81,82,83
Trepper, T. 72,74,79,80,81,82,83
Trostle, J. 132
Turk, D. 130,132,134

Ulman, R. 52
Umbarger, C. 151
Urquiza, A. 73
Utada, A. 50

Van Deusen, J. 141
Varni, J. 129,130,131,132,133,134,135
Venters, M. 142
Viale-Val, G. 33,107

Wachtel, E. 9
Wahler, R. 31
Walker, L. 138,139,142
Wallander, J. 129,130,134
Walters, L. 77
Waterman, J. 72
Wattenberg, E. 77
Webb, K. 132
Weeks, G. 57
Weidman, A. 50
Wilcox, K. 129
Whitaker, C. 136
White, L. 37,129
White, W. 89
Williamson, D. 130
Wood, B. 113,139
Woodward, C.A. 110

Zilbach, J. 9
Zimiles, H. 109

Subject Index

Accountability in Family Therapy
  of children 5-6,12-15
  of parents 5-6,15-18
  of therapists 5-6,18-22
Adolescent Substance Abuse
  family characteristics 49-51
  family therapy approaches 51-52
  course of treatment of 53-54
  case example 62-68
Antisocial Children
  family characteristics 35-38
  extrafamilial factors 42-43
  individual factors 39-40
Antisocial-Delinquent Behavior
  definitions 30-31
  assessment of 31-33
  prevalence 31,34

Bulimia
  treatment of 97-102
  symptoms of 92
  characteristics of 92-93
  models of 89-91
  case example 102-105
Bulimic System
  internal factors 91-93
  and the Hyper-Americanized Family
    93-95

Chronic Illness in Children
  case example 143-145
  medical aspects in treatment 134-135
  developmental considerations 135-136
  impact on families 129-130
Contextual Theory 10-12

Incest
  short term effects 72-73
  long term effects 73
  family characteristics 74-78
  treatment 78-81
Internal Family Systems Model 90

School Behavior Problems
  definitions 108
  prevalence 107
  family characteristics 108-110
  school characteristics 108-110
Structural Strategic Therapy
  assumptions 2-4
  general guidelines 152-153
  specific pitfalls 153-155
  with Home-School Problems 112-118
  with Substance Abuse Problems 51-52
  with Antisocial Children 38-39,42
  with Chronically-ill Children 136-143